Smart Skills: Working With Others

Smart Skills: Working With Others

Frances Kay

Legend Business, 107-111 Fleet Street,
London, EC4A 2AB
info@legend-paperbooks.co.uk
www.legendpress.co.uk

British Library Cataloguing in Publication Data available.

ISBN 978-1-78955-005-4
Set in Times

Set in Times. Printing managed by Jellyfish Solutions Ltd

Cover designed by:
Linnet Mattey
www.linnetmattey.com

Legend Business
Independent Book Publisher

Contents

Foreword

Myriads of management handbooks in print purport to provide guidance on the key skills to success and business training manuals also abound. Generally, they suffer from one or both of two defects.

Sometimes, the scope of the book is too broad. Attempting to provide comprehensive advice on all the basic business activities, there is no clear message. Nobody can gain proficiency in every field of marketing and sales, administration, purchasing, bookkeeping and financial management in a short period of time, although those who start their own businesses do need to acquire a working knowledge of most. Other titles fail to distinguish between technical capability and personal skills.

However, there are a handful of personal and interpersonal skills that are essential ingredients for success in any business: the private or public sectors and the professions; large or small organisations; employees, business owners or management consultants. These are the subject matter of the Smart Skills series on which all readers can focus to advantage because mastery of them will surely enhance both job satisfaction and their careers.

Even those working for themselves as freelancers or sole business proprietors depend on good relations with customers and clients, suppliers, colleagues and professionals to be successful. In larger organisations, relationships with senior management and peer groups are crucial to career advancement, as well as sustaining an effective and congenial workplace. Time spent in improving your skills in working with others, whatever the relationship, is seldom wasted. As in her other book in this series, *Presentations*, Frances Kay offers experience-based on no-nonsense advice that is readily assimilated and will apply to your work environment.

In the Smart Skills Series Frances and her fellow authors bring together their know-how of core skills into a single compact series. Whatever your level of experience and the rung of your career ladder that you have reached, this book will help you to audit your personal effectiveness and raise your game when interacting with others.

Jonathan Reuvid

Introduction

People power - the most important skill for a successful career

'We must learn to live together as brothers or perish together as fools'
Martin Luther King (speech at St Louis, 22 March 1964)

Getting along well with others – particularly at work, whether it's your boss, colleagues, staff, clients, customers, or suppliers – is an essential skill. The ability to deal with people effectively is something everyone should be able to do. While most of us can engage reasonably well with the majority of people we encounter, there are perhaps a few characters you'll meet at work that require special handling.

Professional people know that relationships with others can dramatically affect business success and career development. Despite the amazing progress of technology, which enables machines to do almost anything you want, instantly, it is still vital to get on, cope, and fit in with the workplace crowd. From time to time colleagues may behave in a seemingly unreasonable fashion; it is then that your people skills will be needed to help you solve the problem. It is a fact of life, in the ever increasing pressure of the work environment, that other people can be difficult, sometimes even impossible. So it will probably happen to you, if it hasn't already.

Making relationships with colleagues work is more than just being able to communicate well. Of course that matters. But now and then you may find troubleshooting skills necessary (for dealing with unexpected situations and emergencies). While many work-related relationships run smoothly most of the time, when problems occur it can have far-reaching effects on your career, your health and happiness.

Whether you are new to your career or have recently taken up a different position and want to shine, or just need to brush up on your people power, this book will help. The emphasis is on workplace relationships but it will also help you in dealing with others in all sorts of situations. Today many people believe that, with the right qualifications and technical experience, they are well equipped to climb the career ladder. But additional skills, often referred to as "soft skills", come in useful too. Ideally, a balance of technical and people skills is best if you can achieve it. Quite often there just isn't time (due to pressure of work) to build positive relationships with others. But you may need to get on with colleagues reasonably well (and long enough) to get a job done.

If you find dealing with others an uphill task, the more likely you are to encounter difficulties. You could, for instance, come up against someone in a position to influence your career progression. How do you handle them? What skills are needed to ensure they don't ruin your promotion prospects? This book contains advice on acquiring rapport-building skills and how to get the best out of working with others. If you are keen to progress in your chosen profession, it will give you advice and help you on your way.

So why do workplace relationships matter? Because no matter how brilliant you are at your job, if you want to get ahead, good connections at work are essential. Task awareness is fine, and being good at your job is always desirable. But if you can harness this with being respected and popular with your colleagues you will progress further and faster than others who aren't. If you are prepared to tackle this area of self-development and get it right, you will benefit. You may also have the opportunity to influence positively the growth and profitability of your organisation as well as enhance your own career.

Should you have a problem dealing with an awkward person, you are more likely to get a positive outcome if you have sound inter-personal skills to rely on. If you feel rather nervous about tackling this area, that is perfectly natural. You may be moving into unfamiliar territory. This can make even the most confident among us rather apprehensive. Just remember that getting along well with others in the work place isn't difficult or scary once you get the hang of it. Your people power will grow and your self-confidence increase if you follow the steps set out in this book.

At every level in any organisation you are likely to come across people with whom you may have little in common – colleagues, team workers, staff, managers, directors, customers, clients, suppliers. It is quite natural to veer towards those with whom you can get on easily. But it is occasionally necessary to develop the ability to work successfully with those people you'd prefer (if you were brutally honest) to avoid. Developing the skill to handle all types of personalities, both easy and difficult, will make you a huge asset to your company. Bear in mind that you may be able to accomplish tasks quickly, but dealing with people takes more time. When building relationships with people, you simply can't rush things; whereas you can establish rapport with someone quite quickly. We will distinguish the difference between 'rapport' and 'relationship building' in the course of the book.

Working with Others covers issues that are commonly found in the work environment in a user-friendly and down-to-earth way. It is aimed to be simple to understand, in accessible format and there is little jargon and no management-speak. With a modern approach, it is intended to convey know-how as part of the *Smart Skills Series*. These books offer help to those wishing to succeed in their chosen profession and is proving popular internationally with large numbers of readers. Other titles in this series include *Mastering the Numbers, Meetings, Persuasion, Presentations* and *Negotiation*, which complement this volume.

In essence, this book focuses on the wide range of situations and personalities you meet at work. It provides advice and suggestions for getting along with your co-workers and colleagues. You will (if you read through to the end) be able to manage everyone from the charming to the less than charming characters you can't avoid.

What makes such people tick? How is it best to deal with them? How can you overcome the problems and be a winner? Maybe you need to match their methods, be rough or tough it out? The following chapters deal with a variety of issues you will encounter in the work environment. Whatever stage you have reached in your career, this book will be relevant for you.

Working with Others is designed to make it possible for professional relationships to flourish, for careers to progress and for workers to develop congruent communication skills which are advantageous to everyone. It will help you to understand yourself, as well as different types of people. You should, as a result of reading it, enjoy going to work, secure in the knowledge that should conflicts and disagreements occur you will know how to handle them. Harmony is what is needed to give everyone an easier life. After all, most of us spend a large proportion of our lives in the workplace – why not make it a peaceful, friendly and congenial place? That's something to aim for.

Chapter One

How do you present yourself?

'You can tell a lot about a fellow's character by his way of eating jellybeans.'
Ronald Reagan (New York Times) 15 January 1981

When you consider how many billions of people there are in the world, there are lots and lots of different types. Most people you meet are, on the whole, pleasant, friendly, decent individuals. But not always. From time to time people encounter colleagues at work who are anything but easy. As a starting point however, where working with others is concerned, it pays to know yourself reasonably well. What makes you tick, how reasonable are you and do you come across well to other people? So this chapter is all about you (not *other* people).

For instance, take a moment to consider the following:

- Do you get on reasonably well with others?
- Are you fairly extrovert and find it easy talking to people you've just met?
- When you are working with someone you don't get on with, are you almost certain it is the *other* person's fault?
- Are they, in your opinion, 'unreasonable'?
- Do you wonder what is causing it?

These may seem odd questions, but maybe you've bought this book because you are convinced that it is *other* people who are difficult to work with.

- Can you be sure you haven't ever been a nuisance or awkward?
- Do you never lose your temper if things don't go your way?
- How high are your levels of patience?
- Would you react with irritation if you were given information that didn't please you?
- How about if you were blamed for something that had nothing to do with you?

It is possible that some of your encounters with other people could be difficult because of your own behaviour towards them. If so, this is fundamentally a question of *attitude*. Attitude is a most important consideration when looking at how to work well and get the best from other people.

Positive v negative

What sort of attitude do you prefer when working closely with other people? How do you feel when you meet a new colleague? What if he gives you a smile and offers a handshake? Add to that clear eye contact, an open face, clean, neat clothing and good grooming? The overall impression is, surely, a professional one, so you'll probably be feeling quite at ease. Why so? Because what he has exhibited are all *positive* attributes.

A *positive* attitude is worth cultivating. Have you any idea why you're likely to prefer this sort of approach when meeting someone for the first time? Perhaps because:

- it is both attractive and reassuring;
- the person you are meeting is enthused with constructive energy;
- he or she wants to present well towards you;
- this in turn encourages a similar response from you.

It's true, isn't it, that people form a swift first impression of someone? It can be as quick as within five seconds of meeting them. You have nothing on which to judge the person apart from what you see. They may well not have had the time to speak a single word to you. So what of this person who's just been described above? Almost imperceptibly, you will be smiling back at them, possibly extending your hand to greet them. Why? Why will you be looking on them favourably and investing positive energy into whatever you are thinking about?

There may be all sorts of different reasons:

- perhaps they are welcoming you to a new department or team,
- you will probably form a favourable impression of the rest of the group;
- you are more likely to look forward to working with them;
- you already feel comfortable and at ease.

If you have already gained the view that here is someone you can relate to, someone who is professional, someone whom you may well be able to trust, that is the sign of an open and honest person. In return, you can allow yourself to relax a little, and respond in a friendly and cheerful way. There is potential for pleasant and rewarding exchanges.

Consider then the converse situation. You meet someone who:

- scowls at you or avoids your gaze;
- their greeting is off-putting;
- perhaps their body language is also careless;
- they are slouching, perhaps look rather scruffy;
- maybe they are careless about their personal hygiene.

What does this all add up to? A *negative* impression. These people could be unhappy, unlucky, lacking in self-esteem or simply ignorant of the impression they are giving. But what you may already be thinking is that you're not going to find it pleasant or easy working with them. You might feel that they are bound to be trouble, if not now, at some point in the future.

Some negative types can simply be angry at the world. They are constantly imagining slights where none exist or are intended. They tend to feel insulted, undervalued and, if they are whiners, complain about the rest of humanity getting at them or treating them unfairly. In fact, their attitude works completely the opposite way to the positive attitude shown by others. The hostile and negative types seem to go out of their way to make it easy for reasonable people to react negatively towards them. They seem to want the satisfaction of their self-fulfilling prophesy: "this is how it always is when I meet new people... no-one bothers to be friendly......"

It is a fact that, if you behave badly or negatively towards people, they can quite easily (and justifiably) react unenthusiastically towards you. So wherever possible, do as you would be done by. People who are optimistic, friendly and attractive will find their encounters with others mirroring themselves. They will see their own behaviour reflected in the people they meet.

Skills, strengths and sincerity

It cannot be emphasised too much: so much depends on attitude and charisma. If your approach is positive, open and appealing, you will encourage those you meet to be drawn towards you in a warm and friendly manner. Reasonableness, politeness, good manners should be the norm. Try to work with others in the best and most positive way you can.

Although this book is written with an emphasis for those who want to get on better with the people they encounter at work, the advice is generally applicable whether inside or outside the workplace. Getting on with others is an essential social skill, which everyone begins to learn while still very young. As the years go by, the better and more successful you become at dealing with others, the greater the chances of smoothing your own path through life. This also makes things a lot easier for those around you, including co-workers.

If you find it difficult, awkward or just plain scary meeting people, working with new colleagues, what can you do? The answer is to develop curiosity.

If you can train yourself to show interest in other people, you will get on far better than if you try to be interesting yourself.

Take it easy, and do it a stage at a time. Can you remember how you gained your balance when you learned to ride a bike? Did someone teach you to ski, skate or swim as a child? Are you able to snow board or water-ski? What was the learning process like? You probably learned quite a lot by observation, watching other people, and being shown the way by someone proficient. Then you started by taking a few tentative steps, made some wobbly attempts and probably fell over or messed up a good few times. You learned by experience and by paying attention to others.

Whoever you are, whatever you do, if you can build good working habits with colleagues you will stand out as an impressive member of your organisation.

Climbing the slippery career ladder is not easy. There is much hard work ahead of you and you will spend many hours in the workplace. Wouldn't it be nice if the majority of that time was enjoyable?

So, from the outset, pay attention to how you feel in the workplace and how other people react towards you. Before anything else, consider the likely expectations of the people you work with. Everyone prefers to work with people they can get on with.

What would your ideal colleague be like? Would he/she be someone who is:

- positive and enthusiastic;
- able to see the big picture;
- capable of achieving your own goals;
- well organised and self-disciplined;
- a good decision maker;
- provides honest feedback;
- fair and doesn't have favourites;
- open-minded and curious;
- a good listener (and available to listen);
- knows and takes an interest in colleagues;
- is a good communicator;
- shows confidence and gives credit;
- keeps people informed;
- acknowledges his/her own mistakes and weaknesses;
- shares experience and helps others

How many of these attributes do you possess? Be honest when you think about it. Let's hope the people you work closely with have some of them too. These skills are the ones that people who want to work well with others should aim to develop. It is an important list, and these skills will crop up from time to time throughout the book.

Make it your business to discover what is most important to your colleagues and boss. It will be time well spent.

Different strokes for different folks

If you're a new employee, or have recently acquired a new job, because of your skills, experience or ability, try not to give out too much information about yourself at first. You will learn far more by saying less. Best advice is to keep quiet and listen. Smile and let others do the talking (to you). You might try to figure out the office hierarchy by observation. It certainly won't be the same as is shown on the organisational chart. Read anything and everything you can lay your hands on in the early days, should time permit. When joining a team, treat everyone equally. If you are given the opportunity to have extra training, accept it. Everything you learn is going to come in useful one way or another.

You may be starting a new job, but what if it's not your first? Are you being promoted by your current employer or moving on to a new organisation? Assuming it is the former case, you should remember that people already know you. But your position in relation to others will, and should, change. You are actually moving on while staying put – if that doesn't sound like a paradox. Because of your new role, you may have to create a bit of "distance" between you and your former colleagues. Existing relationships and friendships shouldn't dictate the way things will work in future. You may be part of the same team, division or department, in which case you'll need to give consideration to how you act in future. Don't automatically abandon old alliances because of new circumstances – they will still be useful.

Should you be starting work with a new employer, and a new organisation, your learning curve will be much steeper. Everything will be unfamiliar. Discretion and caution will be the best tactics initially.

Once you start your job there will be lots to get your head around. One good piece of advice is to try to get a meeting with your manager early on. Even if it is just to confirm your role and the priorities. It is well worth setting up an effective communication procedure between each of you as early as possible. You will be able to find out whether he wants you to report to him regularly. If so, what method is best? Be sure to ask appropriate questions – ideally ones which demonstrate your knowledge and intellect. The purpose of an initial meeting is to help you both make the first few days go smoothly.

If you are able to arrange to be introduced to other key people, it will be helpful. Your work is bound to involve contact with others. They could be in another department; they may be above or on the same level as you. If you can do a bit of research and come across as being fairly well informed about them, what they do and how they fit into the organisation, this will show that you have a positive approach. It will help you to cultivate a good working relationship from the outset.

When you're new to a position, don't be afraid to ask questions. It is probably the one and only time when most people will be prepared to freely offer you advice and information. Find out what issues are important to them and what they would most like to get out of working with you.

With a bit of preparation, you will create impact wherever you go and with everyone you meet. This will get you off to a good start. Put simply, this means:

I Involve yourself in social activities with colleagues.
M Manage your time effectively while at the office.
P Present yourself well (appearance, body language, voice).
A Ask appropriate and intelligent questions, then listen to the answers.
C Contribute ideas if invited to do so.
T Think – pause for breath before you speak.

You will need to allow time to get to know your colleagues – how they work, their strengths and weaknesses. This can't be done in five minutes.

While some tasks can be accomplished quickly, people-related activities take a little longer.

When properly managed, working relationships can be extremely rewarding. Don't be put off if some people are particularly nervous of change. They may be shy, insecure, feel threatened by newcomers, or envious of your success. You may be feeling exactly the same. Should you be working with someone who has held your position (or a similar one) for a long time, they will want to show a bit of control, no matter how senior (and new) you are. Observation and information-gathering are crucial; you must watch how other people work and interact. If it seems that one or two colleagues are being difficult, they are probably just trying to make themselves noticed. It's quite possible that once they are more used to you they'll feel less threatened and calm down.

The reason why it is so important for you to establish good working relationships with colleagues is because so often you will be reliant on others to help deliver projects, or achieve results. The first step is not to annoy other people just by the way you come across. Developing workplace relationships takes time, because you are trying to develop trust, earn respect and build up confidence. If possible, build rapport with them at the earliest opportunity. Show colleagues from the outset that you are "on their side" and keen to understand where they are coming from. They are then more likely to become allies and, in time, friends.

Another important thing to remember, if you want to make a positive impression on others, is to be (personally) well organised. This should give you a head start in everything you do. Productivity, effectiveness, hitting targets – all important aspects for your work – are improved by good strategy, preparation and planning. Anything less hinders achievement and promotes a view that you are not efficient, giving the impression that you are led by events rather than directing your own destiny.

It always helps to have a plan. The acronym SMART is often used in business coaching. It helps you develop a method for personal organisation which in turn will create a favourable impression on others.

S **Set task times:** Decide how you will organise your working week/day. If you need a day a week to be at your desk, block one out – avoid meetings that take you out of your office. Check with co-workers that this work pattern will fit in with them.

M **Make goals:** Clearly defined objectives help focus the mind and keep you motivated. Avoid setting yourself unachievable deadlines.

A **Ask for help:** Never muddle through. Ask the advice of colleagues who may have previous experience. Enlist expertise of others whose skills complement your own.

R **Reflect:** Rather than reacting. Avoid committing to anything until you have all the facts – a hasty decision could lead to unnecessary stress.

T **Think – use your brain:** Don't open your mouth without engaging the brain. Never be afraid to say you don't know something if you are stumped. Far better to be honest than be found out later on.

To be well organised and efficient you should strive to make the most of your personal strengths. Make sure you behave in an appropriate and professional manner at all times – be polite, punctual and keep up to date with your work. Every aspect of your work can be made more effective if you organise yourself and prepare efficiently. It may need some thought; it may even be difficult. Being self-disciplined is a good habit to develop early on. It will help you as you progress and assist in developing professional working relationships.

Successful integration into the workplace, where you are new to a job or the profession as a whole, requires thought and preparation. Find out as early as possible what the do's and don'ts are in your work environment. If there's a staff handbook available read it and become familiar with it. If in doubt about any aspect of it, ask the HR department for clarification.

Start as you mean to go on, with a positive attitude and the intention of doing the best you can. Once you are confident about who *you* are within the organisation, you can look towards building relationships with others.

Self-management and being effective

No serious professional ever strives to be ineffective. But why are some people considered effective and command respect and loyalty, while others are not? Being effective isn't just about being organised, or self-disciplined. Nor is it about getting things done on time and within budget – even if those are elements of your work on which you can be judged. An effective person is highly motivated and keeps the broader picture in mind whilst inspiring colleagues and employees to excel in their work.

For some this comes easily. They have natural charisma and style and people admire them. But, for others, however competent they are in their professional expertise, they do not easily command respect, loyalty or trust. They need to develop their own natural communication style before they can develop positive workplace relationships. Being effective is based on the ability to keep an open mind and learn from others. If you are ready to accept responsibility and be accountable for your own actions, you are likely to be able to work well with others.

Do you know how you are viewed by your colleagues, staff, partners or directors? Why not try a bit of informal feedback through the team and departments you are already working with? You may be encouraged by what you hear. If the results are a bit negative – don't worry.

Have a look at the words on the left hand column of the effective behaviour checklist below. Are any of these (or similar) likely to describe you? If so, you may need to work towards being more like the words on the right hand column. These encompass positive attributes. The more ticks you get in the right hand column, the better. For future reference, when trying to establish rapport with colleagues, the less negative traits they possess, the easier it will be.

Negative – ineffective	**B E H A V I O U R**	**Positive – effective**
Evasive	**E**	Encouraging
Faltering	**F**	Forward thinking
Frustrated	**F**	Fun
Enigmatic	**E**	Experienced
Critical	**C**	Confident
Troublesome	**T**	Trustworthy
Insincere	**I**	Interested
Visionless	**V**	Visionary
Egotistic	**E**	Enthusiastic

You may be wondering why this is being described here. Because it is so important, that's the reason. Should you be unaware of the negative impact of your, or someone else's behaviour, the sooner you pick up on it the better. If the behaviour isn't yours, but someone else's with whom you work, being able to recognise it will help you to avoid picking up those traits yourself. Perhaps you can recall colleagues with whom you've worked recently who you'd regard as ineffective? Do the words on the left hand column of the second checklist below seem appropriate when describing their actions?

Negative – uninspiring	B E H A V I O U R	Positive – inspiring
Indifferent	**I**	Imaginative
Nervous	**N**	Natural
Suffering	**S**	Sympathetic
Pressured	**P**	Punctual
Insipid	**I**	Impressive
Rigid	**R**	Relaxed
Embarrassed	**E**	Efficient

Consider the words connected to 'EFFECTVE' and 'INSPIRING' above.

If you were to assess your behaviour at work, negative and positive (left hand and right hand columns), how do you think you would rate? What do think those around you, who work with and for you, think about your attitudes and approach in the work place? When seeking feedback you will need to consider: what insights has it given you? What surprises did you get (if any)? Were they good, bad, ugly or interesting? What areas do you need to improve?

After receiving feedback, you should have a better idea of your talents and skills, those areas you are most appreciated in, and the ones you need to freshen up.

Going back to self-analysis, some questions you could ask yourself are:

- how do you like to be managed?
- what skills do you need to be able to do your job?
- what support would help you?

To be effective, you (and your team if you are part of one) need to be focused and working with purpose. If you are currently involved on a project, how would you classify yourself and your team?

High focus, low energy	=	disengaged		
Low focus, low energy	=	procrastinating		
High energy, low focus	=	distracted		
High energy, high focus	=	purposeful	=	positive results

Some people are driven to perform 100% in the workplace, and expect everyone around them to sustain that level of effectiveness as well. Over and above that, sometimes you will have to manage yourself and inspire others to give wholly of themselves. This is a tough one to deliver, unless you're able to show by example that you always give yourself totally to your job. It isn't a question of staying at the office for extra hours, working over the weekends, or being too busy to take holidays.

To sustain the "high energy, high focus" approach you need the best means of working effectively during office hours while leading a balanced life outside the workplace. This will gain you the respect of your colleagues and put you in the best position to work well with others.

How do you come across?

If you want to get along with colleagues, clear communication is key. Misunderstandings can and will occur from time to time at work. In most cases it is because of a lack of clear communication. Most people assume it is the *other* person's fault. If you want good rapport with colleagues you should communicate in an unambiguous way. Could what you say, your manner or style of speech, ever cause a misunderstanding?

Communication is the successful transmission of an idea from one person's mind to another's mind. It is quite often a process fraught with obstacles. All sorts of problems can occur, such as:

- a lack of concentration;
- a perceived prejudice about the communicator ;
- false assumptions about the message;
- dislike of the communicator ;

To be clear and unable to be misunderstood is the ideal. If someone wants to misinterpret what you are saying, there are always opportunities for them to do so. It is not surprising that communication often goes wrong. One study showed that, on average, people leaving an hour-long business meeting had three to four major misconceptions about what had been agreed.

Have you ever been in a situation when working with others where you've hit a communication barrier? This can be extremely dangerous. You may have invented reasons and excuses to convince yourself that the problem had nothing to do with you. Success or failure where communication is concerned is often the result of the attitude of the individual. Whether you are the "transmitter" or "receiver", a change of attitude can bring about an outstanding reversal of results.

The most successful communicators are deeply motivated individuals. It is rare to find successful people who have become successful by doing what they hate or dislike in life. Where there are problems of communication, it is often the recipient of the communication perceiving it to be negative that causes the upset. You may consider someone difficult to get on with if they are delivering ideas that you either don't like or agree with.

In a situation where the automatic reaction is to feel negative towards what is being communicated, remember to:

- pay attention, listen, duplicate and understand;
- make no assumptions;
- listen for any free information;
- acknowledge their ideas, repeating the essence if necessary;
- ask a question to ensure that communication is clear or satisfactory;
- if not, identify the expectations before concluding the exchange.

If you communicate with people fairly, in an open minded way, there should be less opportunity for misunderstanding. This may not always be the case, but you should aim to be responsible in the way you communicate with others.

Clear communication comprises:

- Showing interest in the other person by using their name.
- Showing empathy. Remember your own experiences of when you

have been misunderstood or needed clarification.

- Consider the possibility of human error. You don't want to be misheard or misrepresented. Make sure they have all the facts.
- Take responsibility for the communication.

If you are trying to explain something which is difficult, keep language as simple as possible. Remember, when communicating, people won't always agree with you. Take each and every opportunity to listen and acknowledge. Effective and positive communication begins with recognition and appreciation that each party has a right to hold different views. It is helpful if you can tone your body language and voice to be as neutral as possible.

An atmosphere of trust, confidence and participation is essential when trying to work well with other people. They need to feel able to respond freely. Body language and tonality are most important. People who are getting on well tend to mirror and match each other in posture, gesture and eye contact. Their body language is complementary. Successful people create rapport with colleagues and in turn this helps to develop trust.

In the next chapter, we deal with confidence issues, making friends (not enemies) and dealing effectively with colleagues.

Chapter Two

Confidence, Colleagues and Collaboration

'In order that people may be happy in their work, these three things are needed: They must be fit for it; they must not do too much of it; and they must have a sense of success in it.'
John Ruskin

New skills need confidence

Are you thinking that working well with others is proving just a bit more than you bargained for? If you are, it shows that you are taking things seriously and have ambition. No-one ever got anywhere without effort. Your new challenge could take you a step (or two) up the career ladder. Although you will need focus, application, specific approaches and new skills, things can be taken at a steady pace and adjustments made where necessary. This book is designed to help you feel able to deal with each step as you go forward and develop your confidence at the same time.

There is a lot of change involved if you are transitioning from being task aware to becoming more people oriented. People power, interpersonal skills – whatever you call it – even if it is not an entirely new concept for you, requires a different approach. Your decision to work as hard at getting on with people as you have been at dealing with tasks will almost certainly involve developing confidence to cope with the challenges ahead.

Here are a few points to bear in mind. Do you work in the private or public sector? The cultures differences within these sectors are marked.

Depending on where you are employed, it is important to pay particular attention to what is involved in your specific situation. Some organisations are extremely hierarchical, even today, whereas smaller companies can be quite informal. Perhaps you work for a multinational company. This could involve cross-cultural working relationships. As the UK is one of the most multi-cultural nations in the world, and its biggest cities have some of the greatest mixes of nationalities and languages, you could be working with a number of people from across a variety of continents.

Where workplace relationships are concerned, you (and your colleagues) may need time to adjust, particularly if you are in a new job where things are very different from anything you've experienced before. Many organisations offer excellent induction training. Be sure to take advantage of whatever scheme there is. It is designed to take away the fear factor and help you develop confidence in the workplace and among departmental colleagues.

Depending on your level of seniority, your training manager, or HR director, is the person to turn to for help and advice. Some organisations offer formal "induction" programmes. You may have a number of "meet the people" series of events arranged. The induction timetable is adhered to until completed, by which time total absorption in the corporate culture and hierarchy should have happened. It is possible (though hopefully unlikely) that you could be thrown in at the deep end and you could be struggling quite soon. If you are not given any induction training, ask if it is possible for you to have some opportunity for this, or at least "job shadowing" from someone familiar with your role. It is only fair that you are given adequate time to adjust to your new workplace and environment.

Where confidence building is concerned, let us continue with the new job theory for a moment. People achieve a new position usually because they are good at something. Did you get your current job:

- because you were particularly **successful** at what you used to do?
- because you have moved to a more senior position within the company?
- or to a new one, doing broadly similar work because you have outstanding **experience**?

- or, did you get your present position because of the **skills** you have?

If you want to be confident at work, the most important issues you face are:

Challenges: do you have enough / too many?
Without doubt the main challenge you face is other people. You may prefer to work on your own, because if for example you are naturally more task oriented, this may be how you got to where you are. But if you are trying to be more confident when working with others, one way of doing this is working as part of a team. Open plan offices are the norm and although people sit closely together but in separate work stations, people are not necessarily interacting all the time. But it is likely that in the course of your work you report directly to others or have staff reporting to you.

Learning curves: do you welcome them/do you learn easily?
One of the best ways to ensure you succeed in your goals is to have confidence in yourself and your skills. If you think the prospect of working well with others as something enjoyable, requiring new approaches and offering you greater challenges, this is a healthy sign. You may have some previous experience (good and bad) but by looking forward, trying to learn fast, you will have the right attitude.

Personalities: how do you cope when there are clashes?
One of the most important things in the beginning is to keep an open mind about your colleagues. Suspend reaction, try not to make assumptions and judgements, or jump to conclusions about systems they use, how they deal with other people or how they run projects. If you can adopt new ideas and ways of approach easily, your actions and attitude will make all the difference between success and failure.

Working with and relating to people requires a confident strategy – there is more to it than just getting on with a task. It is important to remember that tasks can be carried out, skills taught and new habits acquired relatively quickly. Results are what it is all about. But where people are concerned, although you need to find out swiftly and sensitively about their attitudes and personalities, the process is more complex.

Does your position involve a set of **key tasks**? These could be:

- **Planning** (what must be done to achieve the desired outcome).
- **Organising** (yourself, time, other people and activities),
- **Recruitment and selection** (if managing a team or department).
- **Training and development** (your own skills or those of your staff).
- **Motivation** (creating and maintaining a positive attitude).
- **Control** (monitoring your own performance standards and those of others).

Success in these will vary depending on the exact nature of the work you do and how good you are at dealing with other people. It is most likely that you will be expected to be able to take decisions and make them work. You may also have to be good at problem solving, time management, communication and presentations.

There are three things that help you become skilled at working well with others:confidence, knowledge and focusing on the positive.

Confidence: It is easy to feel intimidated and overwhelmed when trying something new. However, if you approach working with others with confidence, you will find that colleagues respond positively. Courses such as public speaking and presentation skills training can help you overcome shyness and build your self-assurance in the early stages. Should your organisation offer anything along these lines, take advantage of any in-house opportunities provided.

Knowledge: One quick-win is to learn people's names. If you've a good memory this will be an easy habit to adopt. If you are new to your job, make time early on to check the company website, or Intranet, regularly for updates. It can be a great resource. All the information you need will probably be found on the Intranet site. Most now include pictures so you can see what people look like. To shine where inter-personal relationships are concerned, collect as much information as possible to have at your fingertips: internal phone directory; speed dialling codes; departmental electronic diary; contact lists; useful phone numbers;

operation manuals, email addresses, working groups and teams names and mobiles.

Once you have done this, socialise as much as possible with co-workers. Accept invitations to after-work drinks, lunches and group events. Arrange coffees and lunches to get to know your immediate colleagues better. If time allows, volunteer to help with work events/corporate functions/charity fund-raisers. The sooner you get involved the better.

Focus on the positive: The greater the inter-personal skills you have directly affects your ability to succeed in your role. Some people believe success in business is 20% strategy and 80% people. If you can communicate well with others (business writing, making effective presentations, running meetings, liaising with staff on a one to one basis, conducting interviews and appraisals), use these skills wherever you can.

Even if you are finding things difficult, make a note of the skills you have and how you rate them. This sort of self-analysis is useful when trying to measure your progress in getting along with others. You may have received feedback on previous occasions and found it accentuated the negative. Employee evaluations tend to focus on opportunities for improvements, with the sting of criticism often lasting longer than the faint glow of praise.

Maybe it would be sensible at this stage to conduct a self-appraisal designed to give you an idea of your progress in developing your people-skills. Perhaps you have a couple of colleagues who could help you do this. Collect some feedback from people who know you well – they could be from inside or out of work. But ask for positive information only on your people skills. When you've spoken to them what are the results? Do they say broadly the same things? Spend a bit of time working out the areas you think you could improve on.

The purpose is to build on what you are already good at and find ways to work on the other areas. By using your strengths you can shape the pattern of progress towards the next phase. Taking action as a result of accurate self-appraisal is a very honest way to help yourself achieve your goals.

Allies are better than enemies

The Pareto Principle, which most of us are familiar with, is applicable here. Pareto's Law (the 80/20 rule) states that 80% of results flow from just 20% of causes. In terms of getting along well with others, this means that you only have to get 20% of what you do right to achieve 80% success. Now that doesn't sound too bad, does it?

So, make it a rule to manage yourself, and work in a way so that you focus on your core 20% of key tasks. Your objective is to have a confident attitude when working with colleagues. If you are required to manage others, try to get them to work in a way that reflects the realities of the 80/20 rule.

The success of your plan depends not only on yourself but your co-workers. Other people are likely to relate positively towards you if you are good at what you do. Going back to the importance of creating a good first impression, do you appraise other people when you first meet them? It does not take long to form an initial view of someone. Most people will:

- **Observe** the person's manner and style.
- **Listen** to what they say, then read between the lines.
- **Watch** what they do and how they do it.
- **Look** at how it affects and relates to them.

It's quite unnerving if you think about this too much. If you are in the position where people are likely to observe your every move, it is important to prepare as well as you can so that you come across as confident and professional. If you're intent on making a good impression on those you work with, **you** have to make it happen. No one else will do it for you.

A good beginning

Success is something that is actively gained, not achieved through good luck. There is a saying "Luck is a matter of preparation meeting opportunity". It is always a good idea to take advantage of any lucky opportunities that come along but, without a success strategy, luck alone will not get you where you want to be. Once you've devised your collaborative strategy you must demonstrate to superiors, colleagues and staff that you are well positioned to succeed.

Your action plan is two fold: yourself and others. Setting up an action plan will help you to remember what needs to be done, how it should be done, when it needs to be done by, and the impact it will have on people. In its simplest form, your action plan could be as follows:

- **Skills** (yours and the people you want to work successfully with).
- **Personality factors** (where there are similarities and contrasts).
- **Knowledge** (of their job, role, organisation, people, product – whatever is relevant).
- **Connections** (who they know may be helpful as well as who you know).
- **Profile** (how they are perceived in the organisation).
- **Attitudes** (how these affect their work and dealings with other people).

If you match this list against your personal strengths, and compare the results with what you know of your colleagues, you will see how things begin to shape up. How do you compare alongside your co-workers? Are any of them at all similar to you or are you total opposites? Are there any complementary areas? Which aspects of your personality give you an advantage? Which ones will you have to curb? What areas of knowledge do you need to extend? How will you do this? Who do you know that might be helpful to you in creating positive workplace relationships?

It might be sensible, when considering your answers, to take a "short-term" and then a "long-term" view. For example, creating rapport with someone is relatively quick. Whereas developing working relationships with colleagues takes longer. You may well have skills that will help you to make some "quick wins" in your action plan. However, building workplace associations based on mutual trust and respect takes time, so patience will be necessary.

Your personal action plan might be to:

- **Read** everything you can about the people you are working with.
- **Attend** any courses available that relate to developing people skills.

- **Persuading** someone (a member of staff, colleague) to mentor you.
- **Obtaining** permission (from your manager) to attend internal events.

If you can develop the habit of updating your plan weekly or monthly, it will form a progress check in your acquisition of people skills. You need to be aware of what information will help you when working alongside others. You also need to know where you can find it. Here are some things to consider:

- **Targets** (self-imposed personal and group/departmental).
- **Procedures and systems** (what should you be familiar with ahead of time).
- **People** (who is who? How many of them have you already met?).
- **Lines of communication and reporting** (who do you report to and who reports to you; what processes are used – meetings, written reports etc.).

Make notes of everything as you acquire information. The more experienced you become, the easier this will be. What you are trying to achieve is being in the best possible position from your colleagues' point of view, so that any future dealings with them should not be too problematic.

You may feel that you are only just starting on your plan to turn colleagues into allies rather than potential enemies, but let's recap on the reasons why it is necessary to have people skills. What use are they? The simple answer is that there is nothing to be gained from not getting on well with your co-workers. How you make your initial approaches depends entirely on you. Best advice is to start off among your team or department until you get more confident. Wherever you begin your first positive experience may be in the most unexpected place at the least anticipated time.

Say your company sponsors a charity or organises a fund-raiser. You could quite easily volunteer your time and energy in helping out. This is an excellent way of getting involved and making a contribution to a worthwhile charity project at the same time. The more you take part in whatever voluntary work your company encourages its employees to do, the better you'll get to know others who share your interest and desire to "make a difference". This is where the personal touch comes in. You will be far more enthusiastic about working as a volunteer if you have passion for the cause. Many wonderful organisations offer volunteer opportunities but some of these require a serious time commitment. Take into consideration that you will not be paid and these hours will have to be outside of office hours.

If you think that developing strong interpersonal skills will enhance your career, the workplace is the most sensible place to start. You could meet a whole new crowd of people if, for example, you've recently moved to a new office location, or you've just been promoted to another department. Some companies have great opportunities for socialising, so don't overlook anything.

How to win friends and influence people

If you haven't read the famous book, written by Dale Carnegie in the early part of last century, it's still available and well worth browsing through. Certainly for those keen to develop people skills there is nothing more important than being able to make friends with people you work with. Something as simple as a friendly wave or smile as you enter your place of work in the morning can transform it for you in an instant.

Companies prosper when staff are genuinely interested in their colleagues and get along well.

When building good working relationships, it all comes back to confidence. Some people are naturally reticent while others are born extroverts. People who have strong people skills show certain characteristics:

- They treat everyone as being interesting, special and likeable.
- They use good eye contact and positive body language.
- They make other people, particularly new acquaintances, feel special.
- They introduce people to each other effortlessly, remembering names and something relevant about those they introduce.

In other words, they have "charisma". If you are charming it is contagious – you come across as being generous and will be able to build self-esteem in others.

You may have met someone like this already in your career. When you were introduced, they smiled, entered into conversation easily and drew you out. They probably asked you questions about yourself and listened to what you said. In essence, they made you feel important. When you parted, you probably thought to yourself, "What a great person!" Not only is it easy to be in their company, these people are at ease with themselves.

If you work with someone who is highly task aware (or even if you are a bit that way inclined yourself) such people often find it difficult to appreciate the value of personal relationships at all. They are happy to sit at their desk, glued to their computer screen all day. They find it preferable to interacting with other people. As a colleague you are likely to receive an email request from them, rather than a personal approach, even if they are sitting next to you. They may go so far as to avoid the coffee machine in case they get caught up in conversation. Sometimes a bit of staff bonding goes a long way to encourage good relationships among team members and colleagues.

The idea may not have occurred to you because you're too concerned about how you come across, but don't forget your colleagues and your superiors are human beings too. They have hopes, fears and insecurities just like you.

Getting the most from others

If you can cultivate the ability to see the world from other people's perspectives you can then observe your new colleagues work styles. Start by identifying key players.

Influential people.

It is a common assumption that influential people are those who hold high office. This isn't necessarily so. You may find from experience that there are those who are not in elevated positions, or immensely senior, yet they wield considerable power.

Case Study
This is extracted from *Making Management Simple (Change Management)* published by How To Books.

The board of a company decided as part of their modernisation that they needed to join two buildings together which were separated by a busy road. They commissioned architects and consultants to apply to the local planning department to build a bridge between the two factories. The application was refused. They spent many hours and much money researching other solutions but came up with none. The board and the consultants were stuck.

One morning the chairman of the board was driving to work and saw ahead of him the caretaker on the other side of the road. The man disappeared into the building but by the time the chairman passed that spot he saw to his amazement the caretaker standing on the other side of the road. The chairman stopped his car and shouted to the caretaker, "How did you do that? Get from one side of the road to the other without walking across?"

Answer? *There was an underground maintenance passage. For some reason it was not on the building sites plans but it was in daily use by a small section of the workforce.*

Moral: *Never be too proud to ask or underestimate the knowledge and experience of every single person you work with.*

Another example:
Andrew used to work for a global company which was hierarchical in its approach. One day he needed the advice of the Chairman on a particular matter. He went through the usual channels and asked the Chairman's PA if he could possibly see him for ten minutes. She replied that he was not available for two weeks.

Andrew knew the decision could not wait, so he went to find the Chairman's chauffeur. He found him in the company canteen and bought him a cup of coffee. In the course of the conversation he asked Charles, the chauffeur, where the Chairman was that day. Charles told him he was driving him to the airport that afternoon at 3.00pm, and if he wanted to see him he should be waiting by the main entrance.

Andrew was at the door, as suggested, at the appointed time. The Chairman spoke to him, invited him to ride with him to the airport so that he could give the matter his consideration. The advice was given and the problem solved.

Some points to remember:

- Be prepared to think laterally to solve problems.
- Remember a small piece of information can make a huge amount of difference.
- Pay attention to everyone – and discover their individual strengths.
- Sometimes a valuable piece of information can come from the most unlikely source.

Movers and shakers.
These people usually far exceed the boundaries of their office positions. When developing people skills it is a good idea to find out who they are in your organisation. You won't have trouble spotting them because they make it their business to know everyone and be seen. Movers and shakers are important to keep track of – you never know where they are going to turn up next.

Corporate citizens.
These are hard-working, non-political types, who are great sources of information and advice on almost everything to do with the organisation. They have probably been around a while and know all the details of the company, their department and most of the personnel. They probably even know the date of the CEO's wife's birthday. You can always ask their advice when appropriate and they'll probably be happy to help. Better to ask them than have them saying afterwards, "If only you'd asked me, I could have told you that……"

Sometimes colleagues fall into categories. These are fairly broad-brush descriptions, but you may be able to recognise some similarities among colleagues and other personnel:

- **Road runners:** are often highly task aware and don't want anyone to get in their way of achieving targets. It is wise to let them go at their own speed because if you try to get involved it will only slow them down.
- **Race horses:** get things done fast but like others alongside to help them. They are perfect to team up with because of the accelerated pace at which they work. If you join them you will find yourself flying along. A racehorse is a valuable asset in any group. They are strong and capable and can achieve great things but work best when there is someone in charge of the reins.
- **New Pups:** are the most people-oriented types and will be so eager to get to know you. They like working with others but have a tendency to forget the importance of getting things done. They sometimes spend too much time being helpful and friendly when they should be concentrating on their own work.
- **Tom Cats:** prefer to work on their own. As colleagues they can be rather hard work. They are independent and don't regard other people and teams as very important. Some of them produce the most amazing results, but can be remote figures and content in their own company.

In the workplace you will find that your co-workers have different energy levels. There is a theory that people can be represented by a colour. What colour are you and your colleagues? There are four main types:

- **Cool blue** – they are usually regarded as stand-alone types. They can be cautious, precise, deliberate and formal. If they are a bit distant, it's nothing personal. If you are trying to work with them, you will need to work on them slowly.
- **Fiery red** – these are pretty much the opposite of the blues. They are competitive, demanding, determined and strong willed. They will reach their goals whatever it takes. Sometimes they would do better to tone down their actions because they can easily overwhelm colleagues.
- **Sunshine yellow** – sociable, dynamic, demonstrative, enthusiastic and persuasive. The yellows are an asset to any organisation, have

natural charm and are able to shine in any situation. They help keep morale high among colleagues; no matter how difficult their job is, they see things in a positive light.
- **Earth green** – these are the caring, sharing, encouraging, compassionate and patient individuals. If you've got any greens in your workplace, they're the ones who always have the headache tablets and bandages; they water the plants and remember everyone's birthdays.

If you want to work well with people who are not like you, you could try adopting the chameleon approach – change colour to suit the environment you're in.

Chapter Three

The art of communication

'Good communication is as stimulating as black coffee,
and just as hard to sleep after.'
Anne Morow Lindberg, American Author

What is communication? In short, it is signalling. The transmission, by speaking, writing or gestures, of information which evokes understanding. That's simple enough, isn't it? It's straightforward in theory, but in practice often fraught with difficulty. This is particularly so when you are not experienced and you want to come across well in front of colleagues.

But it is more than the transmission of information. Something else has to occur for the communication to be complete. In essence – the other parties to the communication method have to engage the brain and receive the message. When dealing with work colleagues this is not always as simple as it seems. There are plenty of opportunities for misunderstanding and miscommunication for the inexperienced. You will observe that people with strong people skills are almost always good communicators.

What happens when you open your mouth? If you manage to insert both feet with speed and agility, you're probably just a bit nervous. Don't be surprised if words come out which you seemingly have no ability to control. A conversation under these circumstances can go seriously wrong before you've had time to do much more than sit down.

There are some points to remember when considering the various methods of communication and some hazards to be aware in the initial stages.

Only 7% of the impact you make comes from the words you speak and that 7% comprises:

- the type of words you use;
- the style of sentences;
- how you phrase them.

If you want to make a favourable impression with your colleagues, consider the words, the ideas and structure of the message you wish to convey. Keep it as simple as you possibly can. Always aim for clarity over ambiguity. Some useful tips:

- Commonly used words, in short, direct sentences, have the greatest impact and allow the least margin for error or misinterpretation.
- Long words wrapped in complex sentences are confusing and best avoided. Don't use jargon either – unless you are sure it will be understood by all those present.
- Positive statements are far more acceptable and will gain you greater advantage than negatively expressed remarks.

Using your voice effectively can help you get your message across. Tone, inflection, volume and pitch are all areas to consider. Relatively few people actually need to develop their speaking voices, but many do not understand how to use it effectively. The simplest way is to compare the voice to a piece of music – because it is the voice that interprets the spoken word.

If you've had some training in public speaking, perhaps you've come across the following mnemonic: **RSVPPP**. It is useful as a memory jogger for optimum vocal effect.

R Rhythm
S Speed
V Voice
P Pitch
P Pause
P Projection.

Rhythm: Speaking without tonal variety can anaesthetise your listener. Try raising and lowering the voice to bring vocal sound to life (and keep your audience awake). Rhythm is directly linked with speed.

Speed: Speed variation is connected to the vocal rhythm. Varying speed makes for interested listeners and helps them maintain concentration. If you're recounting a story, speed helps to add excitement to the tale. But the speed of delivery should be matched with the volume you're speaking at.

Volume: Level of volume obviously depends on where the conversation is taking place. It would be inappropriate to use loud volume when speaking in a one to one situation. However, you'd probably need to increase it if you were talking in a crowded venue, such as a business reception or work area. Volume is used mainly for emphasis and to command attention – lowering your voice can add authority when telling an interesting story or giving advice.

Pitch: Pitching your voice is something public speakers do. They are trained to "throw" their voices so they can deliver their speech clearly to their audience in whatever size or shape of the room they're speaking in. In general, it's irritating to any listener if they have to strain to hear what the speaker is saying. In normal conversations where you need to be heard clearly (for example in restaurants where there is continual background noise as well as the hubbub of other voices) it's impossible to pitch your voice if you hardly open your mouth to let the words out. Correct use of mouth, jaw and lip muscles will produce properly accentuated words and assist with clear enunciation. Pay attention to these facial muscles otherwise your voice will be just a dull monotone.

Pause: Practice the pause. It can be the most effective use of your voice though it is often ignored. A pause should last about four seconds. It sounds like an eternity perhaps but anything shorter will go unnoticed by your listener. You can use the time to maintain good eye contact. The effect can be dynamite. Remember the "er" count. Filling spaces in conversation with props such as "ers", "ums" or "you knows" where there should be pauses are clear signs of nervousness.

Projection: This encompasses everything about the way you come across: power, personality, weight, authority, and expertise – what some people call "clout". You want to build some powerful professional connections. It pays to have gravitas in your dealings with people. Projection is an art which can be practised. But you can learn a great deal from listening to experienced communicators who are experts in these skills.

Remember, your voice is an instrument – just like your body and it is flexible. You know the expression "It's not what you say, it's the way that you say it". That couldn't be more true. Keep in mind the following:

- **Be clear** – use simple, easily understood words and phrases.
- **Be loud** (enough) so that your listeners can hear you.
- **Be upbeat** – a bright and confident tone will inject interest into what you're saying Do stop for breath. Your listener will need to digest what you've said – and to have the opportunity to respond.

Listening skills

The key to success is to get on your co-workers' wavelengths as soon as possible. By putting yourself into their shoes you'll demonstrate your ability to empathise with them. They'll find communicating with you easier and respond positively. One of the most important aspects of communicating is to develop good listening skills. Lots of people are bad listeners. You are not alone if you are far more interested in what you have to say than what the other people are saying to you. Poor listening damages potentially useful exchanges and that is what you should be at pains to avoid. Good listening, on the other hand, avoids misunderstandings and the errors that result from them. The behaviour of a good listener is as follows:

- An attentive listener keeps a comfortable level of eye contact and has an open and relaxed but alert pose. You should turn towards the speaker and respond to what he is saying with appropriate facial expressions, offering encouragement with a nod or a smile.
- Becoming a good listener will help smooth working relationships with others. It requires a degree of self-discipline and a genuine desire to take on board the message the speaker is trying to convey. You need to be able to suspend judgement and avoid contradicting

or interrupting them. Postpone saying your bit until you are sure they have finished and you have understood their point.

Reflecting and summarising: this involves you repeating back a key word or phrase the speaker has used. It is one way of showing you have listened and understood. Summarising gives the speaker a chance to add to or amend your understanding. Your colleagues are far more likely to listen to you if you let them know you've heard what they've said by using these tactics.

Pitfalls to avoid include thinking up clever counter arguments before the speaker has finished making their point. Don't interrupt unnecessarily or react emotionally to anything that is said. If the subject becomes dull or complex, don't register your disinterest by succumbing to distractions or fidgeting.

The five levels of listening skills

Level 1: The first and worst level is ignoring the speaker.
You look away, avoid eye contact and do something else altogether. This is dreadful in a business context. Your colleagues will never give you the time of day again if you commit this cardinal sin.

Level 2: The second level, which is almost as bad, is to pretend to listen.
This can be fraught with danger. If you're nodding your head, and saying "mmm, yes, aha" when you actually have no idea what's being said, you could be in for a nasty shock. Don't be surprised if you hear your colleague saying, "So you'll run in the London Marathon next year on behalf of my favourite charity – how wonderful."

Level 3: The third level listening skill is being selective.
You may well find yourself listening for key words that are of importance, such as "salary increases", "ten per cent" or "Christmas bonus". The result is that you could miss the context of the exchange. Your colleague could have been telling you that none of these are happening at the moment due to the economic down-turn.

Level 4: If you can develop the fourth level skill, you're doing well. It is attentive listening.
You are focused, with positive body language, leaning forward, nodding your head appropriately and maintaining eye contact. The other members of the group know you're paying attention. This creates an atmosphere where they'll want to share valuable information and engage in serious dialogue.

Level 5: The final level is empathetic.
This is the ability to put yourself in someone else's place and see things from their perspective. It is the art of being able to identify mentally and emotionally with your communicator; fully comprehending the tones, pitch, body language and other subtle messages they are conveying. This takes time to achieve but it will impress anyone once you have reached it.

Directing the communication cycle
What about a situation where you are seeking information from colleagues? It's easy to ask too many questions and fall into a sort of "Spanish Inquisition" situation. Conversely, when responding to a question, you can give away too much information. If you're on the receiving end of this from your colleagues, you might feel you are being "pumped" for information. It's infuriating and you may want to distance yourself as quickly as possible.

Only one person at a time can truly direct a conversation. One leads and the other tends to follow. This doesn't mean there's no give and take. Neither does it mean that the other party is subservient. But one of the parties should lead and there is merit in you being the one that does so, if your objective is to be in control.

At the start of the face to face meeting, there are usually some general opening remarks. This should take no longer than a few minutes at the outset of proceedings. Watch for the moment when the chatter should cease because if you don't seize the moment other members of the team may lead you off into uncharted waters. Then you may find it difficult to get the conversation back on track.

Someone usually starts off by saying, "Right, shall we move on? Can you tell me..." That person could be you. You may have anticipated the conversation and have a mental agenda. (If it was a formal exchange of information it might be helpful for both parties if it were written down.) Perhaps you've already aired the topics for discussion in a telephone call or email beforehand. There is no rule here, but if something has been agreed it does mean that the exchange should proceed along the agreed lines.

It also provides an element of control during the dialogue, if the conversation meanders into other areas. You could refer back to your brief by saying something like, "We were going to discuss X next......" and then move on smoothly to the next stage. Such exchanges are key to your confidence building. You'll feel better if you get off to a planned start and keep the conversation productive.

To develop a balanced style of communication, you will find it helps to use the following method. There are four stages to a successful exchange.

- Try to begin the conversation by introducing yourself and giving some personal information, your position and something about the brief. This is called the **inform** stage.
- Once you've given this, you could ask a direct question of other colleagues. This is called the **invite** stage. Then wait for his response.
- On receiving this, **listen** to every word.
- Then **acknowledge** and, if necessary, repeat the essence of their response.

If you achieve this cycle of communication you can replay it many times over during the encounter. It will establish good rapport between you and the other parties. It should make the time pass relatively painlessly and result in a positive outcome.

When attempting to get closer to your team members by means of good conversation, pay attention to the importance of **eye contact**. Appropriate eye contact is essential. If you are talking, check that the rest of the group are paying attention. They should be looking at you, nodding occasionally and maintaining an alert and open facial expression.

Things don't always go to plan. Should one of your colleagues appear to be falling asleep during one of your conversational gambits, it could mean: he's had a late night or an early start; he's suffering from jet lag; the atmosphere in the room is too stuffy; or your dialogue is rather boring. Don't wait until his head falls forward and hits the desk. If you fail to notice until you hear the crash, you're definitely talking too much.

Keep an eye out too for **fidgeting;** this could indicate: you've lost his attention; he wants a break; he's irritated by something you've said; or he finds the conversation irrelevant. Whatever the reason, it's time to shut up. Close mouth without delay and smile. Hopefully with a bit of silence you can retrieve a conversation that may have got off to a rather inauspicious start.

Should one of your colleagues start **shaking his head**, this could mean: he wants to say something; he doesn't agree with you; or he simply hasn't a clue what you're waffling on about. Again, as above, time to bring your remarks to a swift close. If you think you've lost his attention completely, and he turned off, try to regain it by asking him a pertinent question. Re-establish eye contact and vary the volume or expression in your voice.

Other forms of communication

Telephone calls: These can be difficult to deal with and can often cause trouble when people don't know each other all that well. First, because you can't see each other face to face, you have to rely on tone of voice. This can be deceptive. He may sound disinterested because he's talking in a low voice. It may be something as simple as the fact that he's got a sore throat, or he's trying to avoid the rest of the office hearing his conversation.

It's essential to pay attention when a colleague calls. If he's on a mobile, you may well get a distortion, due to background noise, traffic, airport announcements or similar. If possible take the phone call in a private place so as to avoid even more noise coming from your end of the phone.

Voicemail: There's an art to leaving successful messages. Be clear and concise. Don't speak too fast. If you are leaving your telephone number, slow down. Speak slowly while leaving the information. If the message is either gabbled or garbled, it will be impossible for anyone to return your call. It helps to state a date and time too, so that the other party can respond quickly if time is critical.

Text messages: the perfect form of communication for quick exchanges of information. One word of warning – don't use confusing abbreviations. If you received the following message about going to a theatre performance– 'CU 7.30.' Does that mean, 'See you at 7.30pm', or 'Curtain Up at 7.30pm'? Check if you are in doubt.

Written communication: The main point about written communication is that whatever form it takes, the recipient cannot see you or hear you. Your colleague has no option but to accept what they read. You should pay particular attention to wording and expressions because if it is at all ambiguous, it is liable to be misinterpreted.

Letters: handwritten letters should be legible. Think of your recipient. Write neatly and clearly and make sure your spelling is correct. It helps to use a decent pen and good quality paper. With a personal thank you note, use a business address because it is a workplace relationship, even if you are thanking him for inviting you to a social occasion. Keep the message simple and make it easy to read.

E-mail: So much has been written about email etiquette, because it is universally the most popular and efficient form of communication. Always check you have the correct email address. If it is a company email, be circumspect. They don't always get opened by the intended recipient directly. Consider the likelihood that your email could be read by someone else; so be careful.

On a more practical level, email is not the medium for rambling on and on about any subject; it should be clear and to the point. It's no substitute for face to face contact, but it does allow for a fast exchange of information, particularly when confirming meetings or referring to matters just discussed.

Being persuasive
Politeness among business associates is always desirable but sometimes lacking. Being courteous to colleagues, co-workers, staff and clients will significantly influence relationships in the workplace and foster a harmonious culture. Hopefully you are not a troublesome character, but go out of your way to deal pleasantly with others. It is important to preserve other people's dignity and respect, particularly if you are keen to develop strong inter-personal skills. The colleague who rides roughshod over other people's feelings in a team (however well he is regarded professionally) does often end up with a load of headaches – mainly caused by his own actions.

Non verbal communication: If you are familiar with the practice of non-verbal communication it can be used effectively to soften the hard-line position of others:

S smile
O open posture
F forward looking
T touch
E eye contact
N nod

If you approach someone with a smiling face, it encourages a similar response from them. Just as important is your presentation and body language. The posture should be open, head upright and you should stand straight but with hands relaxed by your sides. Make appropriate gestures to show that you are welcoming the exchange.

Eye contact should at all times be honest and open. Avoid staring but maintain a steady gaze when speaking to colleagues. At the same time, encouragement by nodding your head shows consensus and indicates that you are taking note of the points being made.

Polite behaviour should ensure smooth interaction between colleagues working on a team or project. If you practice giving the right signals, with luck, others will mirror your actions. Should your department be packed with people who are backstabbing and politicking, this could spell difficulty ahead. Sometimes a working atmosphere worsens because of a new arrival. Some people do seem to act as virus spreaders – the ones whose presence bring a chill factor which spreads like an epidemic. Maybe one of your colleague's approaches needs a makeover? It is easier to adapt an individual's manner when dealing with others, than it is to alter an endemic organisational culture. If the problem is not too great to be rectified, a little praise goes a long way towards helping with these issues.

Maintaining good morale

A morsel of praise rarely goes amiss in the workplace. One of the keys to retaining goodwill among colleagues is to foster a sense of camaraderie. The more control team members have over how, when and where their work is done, the happier they will be. Their performance improves, along with their morale. There is less confrontational behaviour – in short, everyone gains.

Regardless of advances in mobile technology, some things are in danger of becoming too impersonal and remote. There is nothing more encouraging than some good manners and a bit of personal attention. Where a plague of bad behaviour or ill manners pervades the workplace, there is bound to be a deterioration in behaviour among colleagues.

If someone is showing signs of anxiety, stress or depression, they are probably feeling inadequate and undervalued. Left unchecked, this situation could spiral towards absenteeism. Work-related anxiety has knock-on effects because it doesn't go away if you ignore it. Although dealing with anxiety is best done by seeking professional help, starting with a little kindness can go a long way to combat the effects. Helping colleagues cope with challenging situations by praising them can alleviate anxiety symptoms.

Professional colleagues whose motivation levels are high are not likely to be suffering lack of self-esteem or stress. Should grumpiness pervade the workplace, pay careful attention. If you are able to dispense honey rather than vinegar, you might influence your colleagues towards a change of mood. Smiling is the first step and being positive should help to encourage a warmer atmosphere. Beware the chill factor – should moody people be allowed to simmer, you will find this contaminates a team fairly swiftly. The benefits of working with good-tempered colleagues are high. Befriend the difficult ones if you can. It makes it much harder for them to be unpleasant if you're nice to them.

How to handle meetings

Getting the most out of meetings is important, because if they are not constructive, they can be an immense waste of valuable time. Good effective meetings do not just happen. Everyone in an organisation needs to work at it and everyone's role is important – whether they are running it or attending. To get the best out of a meeting it needs to be planned. Meetings are simply another form of communication. They can:

- inform
- analyse and solve problems
- discuss and exchange views
- inspire and motivate
- counsel and reconcile conflict
- obtain opinion and feedback
- persuade
- train and develop
- reinforce the status quo
- instigate change in knowledge, skills or attitudes

The key role of meetings is to prompt change. For that to happen decisions must be made. Poor meetings can be costly because they waste time, divert attention from more important tasks, slow progress and delay action.

For a meeting to be successful, some questions need to be asked:

- is the meeting really necessary?
- should it be part of a regular set of meetings?
- who should attend?

Ahead of the meeting taking place, a number of things need to be done:

Set an agenda. This is very important. No meeting will go well if the content is simply made up as people go along.

Timing. Set a start and finish time and, if possible, give attendees a rough idea of how long each agenda item should take.

Objectives. Always set a clear objective, so that you can answer the question 'why is this meeting being held?'.

Preparing yourself. If you are attending, read all the papers in advance. Check the details and think about what you will contribute.

Other people. If you are calling the meeting, decide on who should be there (and who should not). Also what roles individuals should have.

Environment. A meeting will go more smoothly if people attending are comfortable and there are no interruptions.

Agenda. This document sets out topics for discussion at a meeting, the sequence in which they will be dealt with and administrative information, such as timing and location. An agenda is best circulated in good time ahead of the meeting.

Chair person. Every meeting needs someone in the chair, that is, someone who directs the meeting. An effective chair person makes sure the meeting is positive, handles discussions and sees that objectives are met. One important rule is that only one person may talk at a time and the chairperson decides who that is. He should start the meeting on time, ensure that everyone has their say, and listen. He should summarise clearly and succinctly and provide the final word.

Attendees responsibility. Everyone attending the meeting must play their part. This involves them thinking about their individual contribution. The key things that make for effective participation in meetings are the following: sound preparation; effective communication and well-handled discussion. Bear in mind, if you are new to this game, that a meeting is a public forum. In other words, you are on show. There may be people unknown to you, senior people or important people, and appearance is a factor.

Discussion. You will be able to perform best during the meeting if you remain alert and concentrate on everything that goes on. Listen to everything that is said. Keep thinking – you may have to adapt your contribution in the light of events. Remain calm and unemotional, even if provoked. Don't get into the habit of leaving a meeting wishing you'd said something.

After the meeting. Minutes may be necessary in some cases, but it does make additional paperwork. Minutes provide: a prompt to action, reminding those who have tasks to accomplish that they should get on with them. They are a tangible link to follow-up discussions (or further meetings). They provide a record of what has occurred, particularly what decisions were made and what action decided upon. They should be accurate, objective, succinct, understandable and businesslike.

As a means of communication, meetings should be taken seriously. They should only happen if they are necessary. Preparation should be businesslike and organised. The chair person should maintain effective control and ensure appropriate participation from everyone attending. Meetings must lead to decisions and actions and be constructive. If they are stimulating as well, they will engender good working practices amongst colleagues.

[For a fully in-depth look at meetings, see another of this *Smart Skills Series*, *Meetings* by Patrick Forsyth.]

Chapter Four

Teamwork

'Coming together is a beginning; keeping together is progress;
working together is success'
Henry Ford

As part of your strategy for working successfully with others, becoming a recognised team player is something you must and should do – without delay. You will not achieve this by being aloof. Aim to become part of the team sooner rather than later. If you want to carry (and be carried) along with the crowd, the best you can do is

- Show leadership qualities;
- Get involved;
- Don't shy away from getting your hands dirty (regularly);
- Know what is going on so that you are able to do all this.

People support those who they feel understand their situation. If you can show that you have experience of being a team player, most co-workers will readily accept you. It is then up to you to make sure you can genuinely play your part and become a willing and active participant.

One way of quickly winning hearts and minds is when a crisis strikes. People will appreciate it if you pitch in when there is an emergency. In an "all hands to the pumps" situation, don't hang back. Get stuck in and don't pick the easiest (cleanest) task. There is nothing more helpful in terms of gaining respect from other team members than willingly taking a turn at making the tea or refuelling the photocopier.

Meeting the team

You may, as part of your interview process if this is a new job, have been asked at some stage to meet the team you'll be working with. But if that didn't happen, how should you best handle it? One way is simply to treat it like another interview. Be as professional as you can and ask questions. The team members will be glad to tell you what you need to know.

Meeting the team isn't just a matter of quickly sizing people up, though that can be very useful. When meeting the team try to be relaxed. Most of them will be your peers and you will be under scrutiny, just as you are checking them out. The team could ask you all sorts of questions; so make the most of the opportunity to be equally inquisitive and observant. If you ask them about their work, you will see how they interact with each other. If you can deduce how the hierarchy operates it will be a help. For instance, is everyone equal? Or is there a "Top Dog"?

If you are joining a big team, they will be working out how your skills can bring an overall improvement to the set up. People will look at you to see how your presence can help them. Individual team members may have different expectations or needs.

This meeting is a two-way process. You want to make a strong impression but trying too hard and not being yourself is not a good idea. If after the initial meeting you have a few worries, ask your boss how he thinks you will fit in with the team. If he has had any feedback from them he should use this opportunity to share it with you.

Working together in a team may be a new experience . If so, it will help if you make this clear early on. Once the rest of the team know, it may encourage them to give you some support and help. Becoming part of a team means becoming involved with everyone in a positive way. Interacting with the rest of the team and being a "player" ensures that together you all succeed. The most important things to identify when you start are the office politics and the personalities of your new colleagues. Remember everyone has a different agenda. Co-workers may try to influence your decisions to suit their own ego.

Find out what is required of you by the team leader, and then work flat out to help achieve those goals. If you can deliver what you say you will deliver, your position within the team will be secure. Much depends on your age, and your previous experience. If there are some things you know you can do well, try to adjust your position in the team so that you can play to your personal strengths. You will not be expected to be brilliant at everything. The organisational structure of a team is important. Who does what, how does one job relate to another, the lines of reporting and communication. This is something you need to find out early on.

To be an effective member of a team, here are a few points about how teams should work:

- The team structure should fit the tasks to be done.
- Any changes should be made on a considered basis.
- Those responsible for the changes should express them in a positive way, otherwise they may be viewed with suspicion.
- The team leader should keep the organisation under review to ensure a good "fit" between the team and its task so that it continues to perform well. (External as well as internal changes or pressures can affect this.)
- Teams sometimes need a bit of fine-tuning – team leaders should keep an eye on tasks, individuals members and the team as a whole

Any, even slight, incongruities about the way people are organised can easily dilute overall effectiveness. Team leaders should not make change for change's sake, but neither should they expect things to remain the same without needing change.

Team Dynamics

A quick and simple way to understand the rules of team work is to focus on the dynamics. When working on a project with a group the following five stages have special significance:

Forming   norming   storming   performing   mourning

Forming the group gets together and agrees the way forward. Often there is a uniting cause or goal that binds the team and starts the process of cohesion.

Norming when the team players have agreed the way forward and resolved the structure of working together, they begin a relationship.

Storming as the team settles down to the task, differing opinions, styles and ways of working become apparent and friction appears. This needs to be addressed.

Performing the working relationship matures and everyone in the team has trust and faith in each other. As a whole, the team perform at their best.

Mourning this fifth step is often forgotten, but when a process of change comes to an end, the goal has been reached, there is a sense of relief. In some cases it also creates a sense of anti-climax and loss.

If you have joined a team as part of a new job, where are you in the various stages of team development? Keep this exercise in mind and review from time to time. When a new person becomes a member of the team, or other developments occur, you may find that the group has to re-form, norm and storm all over again to get the performing to its best level.

Self sufficiency and group dynamics

If a team is organised in the way that its people are suitably self-sufficient it saves time and promotes goodwill. Having responsibility is motivational: people tend to do best those things for which they see themselves as having personal responsibility.

There are two distinct levels of self-sufficiency in how people work:

Involvement can be created in ways such as: consultation, giving good information, making clear that suggestions are welcome and that experiment and change in how people do things is a good thing. This provides the opportunity to contribute beyond the base job.

Empowerment goes beyond simple involvement. Empowerment adds the authority to be self-sufficient (making your own decisions) and creates the basis for people to become self-sufficient on an ongoing basis. In a sense empowerment creates a culture of involvement and gives it momentum.

Together, involvement and empowerment create an environment in which people can have responsibility for their own actions. Responsibility cannot be given – it can only be taken. Thus only opportunity to take it can be given.

Creating a situation in which people take responsibility for their work demands:

- Clear objectives (people knowing exactly what they must do and why);
- Good communications;
- Motivation (to show the desirability of taking responsibility for the individual as well as the organisation);
- Trust (having created such a situation, the team leader should let people get on with things);

A team enjoying involvement in what they do and having the authority to make decisions and get the job done, is the best recipe for successful management and a healthy and contented workforce. To recap, a successful team is one that:

- is set up right;
- responds to the responsibility they have for the task;
- seeks constant improvement (doesn't get stuck "on the tramlines");
- sees their manager as a fundamental support to their success.

A team situation will do better, and is more likely to go on doing better ,than a group of co-workers just "told what to do". The team leader is the catalyst – constantly helping the team to keep up with events, to change in the light of developments and succeed because they are always configured for success.

Motivation matters

"United we stand, divided we fall," is an expression which comes to mind when considering the structure of teams. If you are a team leader, involve people on broad issues. This is motivational for all concerned. Never underestimate team players. Their views can enhance everything – methods, standards, processes and overall effectiveness. Resolve now to make motivation a priority. It makes a huge difference. People perform better when they feel positive about the part they play.

As a motivator, you should:

- recognise that active motivation is necessary;
- resolve to spend regular time on it;
- not chase after magic formulae that will make it easy (there are none);
- give attention to the detail;
- remember that you succeed by creating an impact; its cumulative effect should be tailored to your people.

Your intention should be to make people feel individually, and as a group, that they are special. As team leader, you are expected to make sure that there are enough ideas to make things work and continue working. Make it clear to your people that you want and value their contributions. The key to affecting the "motivational climate" is by taking action to do the following.

Reduce negative influences

Views about many factors potentially dilute the good feelings people have about their jobs. These include: company policy and administrative processes, supervision, working conditions, salary, relationships with peers (and others), impact on personal life, status, security. Action is necessary in all these areas to counteract any negative elements.

Increase positive influences

Here specific input can add strength to positive feelings. These can be categorised under the following headings: achievement, recognition, the work itself, responsibility, advancement and growth. Many things contribute – from ensuring that a system is as sensible and convenient to people as possible, to just saying "Well done" sufficiently often (recognising achievement).

The state of motivation of a group is like a set of balance scales. There are pluses on one side and minuses on the other. All of varying size. The net effect of all the influences at a particular time decide the state of the balance and whether – overall – things are seen as positive, or not.

Changing the balance is thus a matter of detail with, for example, several small positive factors being able to outweigh what is seen as a major dissatisfier.

Obtaining significant motivational results

A team leader needs to make it clear from the beginning that they want their people to have job satisfaction. At an early stage they should:

- **Take the motivational temperature** – investigate how people feel now; this is what they have to work on.
- **Consider the motivational implications of everything you do** – put in a new system, make a change, set up a new regular meeting, think: what will people feel about it? Will they see it as positive?
- **Use small things** – regularly, for example, have they said "Well done" often enough lately. Can they honestly answer "Yes" ?
- **Don't be censorious** – they must not judge other people's motivation by their own feelings. Maybe others worry about things they might dismiss as silly or unnecessary. The job is to deal with it, not to rule it out as insignificant.

If you can create the habit of making motivation a key part of your people-management style, it will stand you in good stead. If you care about people it will show.

Getting the best from the team

Recognise from the beginning that your effectiveness, if you are team leader, depends on the team and the interaction of three separate factors. To be a successful team leader, you must:

- ensure continuous task achievement;
- meet the needs of the group;
- meet the needs of individual group members.

This balance must always be kept in mind (though some compromise may be necessary). Your own best contribution to getting things done is ideally approached systematically:

- Be clear exactly what the tasks are.
- Understand how they relate to the objectives of the organisation (short- and long-term).
- Plan how they can be accomplished.
- Define and provide the resources needed for accomplishment.
- Create a structure and organisation of people that facilitates effective action.
- Control progress as necessary during task completion.
- Evaluate results, compare with objectives and finetune action and method for the future.

There are three checklists which can be used in conjunction with what has been set out above. These apply not only to Team Leaders, but if you are new to team dynamics, they should be useful in helping you to integrate into the group.

Checklist 1. Achieving the task

Ask yourself :

- ❑ Am I clear about my own responsibilities and authority?
- ❑ Am I clear about the department's agreed objectives?
- ❑ Is there a plan to achieve these objectives?
- ❑ Are jobs best structured to achieve what is required?

- ❑ Are working conditions/resources suited?
- ❑ Does everyone know their agreed targets/standards?
- ❑ Are the group competencies as they should be?
- ❑ Are we focused on priorities?
- ❑ Is any personal involvement I have well organised?
- ❑ Do I have the information necessary to monitor progress?
- ❑ Is management continuity assured (in my absence)?
- ❑ Am I seeing sufficiently far ahead and seeing the broad picture?
- ❑ Do I set a suitable example?

Checklist 2. Meeting individual needs

Ask yourself if each individual member of the team

- ❑ Feels a sense of personal achievement from what they do and the contribution it makes
- ❑ Feels their job is challenging, demands the best of them and matches their capabilities
- ❑ Receives suitable recognition for what they do
- ❑ Has control of areas of work for which they are accountable
- ❑ Feel that they are advancing in terms of experience and ability

Checklist 3. Team maintenance

To involve the whole team pulling together towards individual and joint objectives, the team leader should ask if he has:

- ❑ Set team objectives clearly and made sure they are understood.
- ❑ Ensured standards are understood (and that the consequences of not meeting them are understood and approved).
- ❑ Found opportunities to create team working.
- ❑ Minimised any dis-satisfactions.
- ❑ Sought and welcomed new ideas.
- ❑ Consulted appropriately and sufficiently often.
- ❑ Kept people fully informed (about the short- and the long-term goals).
- ❑ Reflected the team's views in dealing with senior management.

- ❑ Accurately reflected organisational policy to the team and in their objectives.

An analytical approach to these areas is the foundation to making the team operation work effectively – and thus getting tasks done effectively.

It is possible (as has been shown earlier) to work successfully with all types of people – the tough and the tender. However, nothing throws a spanner in the works quicker than a team member who runs hot and cold. This problem is at its worst if the team leader shows these traits. Sweetness and light one minute (ready to listen and consult) and doom and gloom the next (just demanding that people "do as I say").

Anyone working in a team environment should adopt a consistent style. For example, let people know that:

- you will always make time for them (soon, at an agreed time, if not instantly);
- you will not prevaricate (decisions may not be made instantly – if they need thought or consultation – but nor will they be endlessly avoided. If there must be some delay, tell people why and when things will be settled);
- make sure people understand how you approach things and what your attitude is to problems, opportunities and so on. While solutions may, doubtless should, be different – your method and style of going about things should be a known quantity.

People like to know where they are and work better when they do.

Negotiating skills

Still in the context of working in teams, workplace relationships can be emotionally demanding. Taking responsibility for conflict resolution, negotiation, forming and sustaining healthy teams can use up huge amounts of energy and time. To deal with all this successfully you need to be aware of your own emotions as well as other people's. If you can project yourself into the other people's shoes you will be able to anticipate their needs.

[For in-depth look at negotiation, see another book in the *Smart Skills Series*, *Negotiation* by Anthony Jacks.]

The previous chapter went into detail about how to communicate well. Being a good communicator is essential should you find yourself involved in conflict resolution. Before you can contemplate sensitive negotiations, you need to be able to interact confidently with people whose opinions differ from your own.

The talent of negotiation is best acquired by practice. Here are a few suggestions to get you started.

"Heads I win, tails you lose" is not a particularly good way of approaching the negotiating table, at least not if you want a successful outcome. Negotiation isn't about you winning and everyone else losing. Good negotiation is about a win-win situation. Both sides should feel that they've got something they wanted, or at least are in a better position than when the process started.

Planning your negotiation strategy is the first step. Think of all the potential objections your colleagues may raise. How do you go about convincing them of the advantages of agreeing with you? Try the following principle:

- describe the situation;
- express how you feel;
- specify what you want;
- clarify the consequences.

There are no guarantees that it will work. If it doesn't, try to discover what went wrong and find a clear way forward. You could either adapt your requests, highlighting further benefits to your plan, or offer another, more suitable compromise.

Unsuccessful negotiation is where one of the parties feels they have conceded too much, given way when they didn't want to, and felt unduly pressured into making a decision that doesn't solve the problem. **This is the "lose-win" situation**. The other side may think they've won and felt good about the outcome. **This is the "win-lose" scenario**. But neither outcome can be considered a success.

Winners / losers

Where there is a winner and a loser in a bargaining situation, this is not real negotiating. The usual result is that the other side will not trust the "winners" and won't want to repeat the experience. There's no point in winning battles if ultimately you lose the war. Negotiation is an interactive and balanced process. It involves:

- The initial stance – the starting point, or first offer, which may be something unreasonable.
- The point of balance – the stage at which a deal can be reached, even though it may not be the "best" solution.
- The win-win negotiation – in which both parties are satisfied and feel comfortable with the result.

Where there is a strong adversarial element, each party will be driving the hardest possible bargain. Each side will be trading something (terms, conditions, price), and give and take is necessary. The best outcome is always to arrive at something that is agreeable to both parties. It becomes a sort of ritual, as the parties involved move towards each other and apart as the process continues. The key factors in negotiation techniques are:

- information
- time
- power

Information: Both parties in a negotiation want to know as much as possible about the other. Clear understanding of both sides allows more accurate and relevant reasons to be put forward in the bargaining process.

Time: This can add pressure to the negotiations, depending on how urgently a resolution is needed. When a deadline is imposed, it removes the situation from the control of the negotiator. This adds stress to an already complicated issue, but deadlines are often negotiable.

Power: Many factors add weight (power) to the ability to negotiate. The two most usual ones are the power of precedent – what has happened in the past – and the power of legitimacy – whether the terms being

negotiated are part of company policy or legitimate in terms of factual evidence.
Negotiation is a constructive process and demands that proposals are made and discussed. It may at times be adversarial but, in the interests of long-term resolutions, the overall aim should be a mutually agreeable outcome. Above all, it is about seeking common ground, which is the essence of good dispute resolution. The parties involved will each have objectives. In order to progress to a satisfactory outcome an agenda should be followed. This will involve:

- **asking** questions and listening to the responses;
- **offering** information;
- **honestly** stating a point of view;
- **bridging** a gulf between parties;
- **treating** the other side with respect.

In terms of building strong inter-personal skills, the negotiation process is an exchange (an advanced form of communication) that involves the presentation of proposals and counter-proposals. First you will need to work out your objectives – a clear idea of what result you want. The second aspect relates to variables – factors that can be varied and arranged in different ways to produce potential deals. In addition, successful negotiation (like dispute resolution) involves using a number of basic techniques. If you can learn these, they will be immensely helpful should you have to tackle more complex situations. Here are some of the more important ones:

- **silence** – a pause may make a point or provoke a comment;
- **attention to detail** – never lose track of progress;
- be **reasonable** – keep tone of voice neutral;
- use **perception** – to read between the lines and identify signals;
- **concentrate** – keep thinking and maintain control;
- **variables** – concessions that either side can make;
- **timing** – deadlines in negotiations are usually flexible.

Negotiating involves the process of making a deal with another party and agreeing terms. It is an interactive and balanced process. Although it may seem adversarial, the overall aim is a mutually agreeable outcome.

Humour

Sometimes laughter can release tension if your negotiation has reached a stalemate. If you can harness the power of amused detachment when trying to get to grips with complex inter-personal issues, it could help take the drama out of a crisis. Having a sense of humour in times of difficulty makes a serious issue less traumatic. Problems are only as bad as you allow them to be.

Humour challenges accepted ideas. Some people have a readily accessible sense of humour, while others do not. Not everyone finds the same things funny, and there are some people who find nothing amusing. This is usually due to a conscious effort to take everything seriously.

You might think being serious at all times makes you seem more important. Having a sense of humour is an asset and a powerful skill when you are involved in resolving inter-personal disputes or conducting delicate negotiations. If you don't take things too seriously, and can laugh at situations, you are proving to the "other side" that you are able to look outside yourself and be objective. You are maintaining a certain detachment between the issues and yourself.

Humour usually provokes a smile rather than outright laughter. It is a liberating force because the burden disappears with a burst of amusement. Your sense of humour is an important resource in negotiating with others. It can be used to take the drama out of a sensitive situation. It can act as a great neutraliser of other people's anger. It is physically impossible to laugh and be angry at the same time. There are a number of examples when humour is a great asset:

- when you have to deliver a difficult message;
- if you want to say "no" without causing offence;
- when a problem is becoming obsessive, you can re-think;
- as a release of tension after hard work, a safety valve;
- during a conflict when there is no sign of a solution;
- to regain people's attention if they have switched off;
- to build bridges, overcome barriers of age, education etc.

Having a sense of the ridiculous can be a huge advantage when involved in difficult workplace relationships. Humour makes people laugh, or at least smile. When you last laughed out loud, was it at something you saw, something you read, or something you heard? You can laugh alone but to be able to amuse others, you have to experience something funny yourself.

Using humour in confrontational situations buys you some time. If you can get the other side to smile or laugh, you have for the moment neutralised the tension in the proceedings. This gives you a moment or two to re-organise your thoughts. Laughter prevents people from losing face and eases the strain in exchanges. If you have to deliver bad news and you can combine it with a comic remark or an amusing statement, it will avoid causing offence.

It also neutralises a possibly aggressive response. Uncontrolled anger is dangerous and can escalate into violence. Skilful use of humour can help you to avoid this. When you are funny, your body language, expression and face light up and it is difficult for others to maintain a hostile attitude.

If you are able to develop sound negotiating skills, these are always in demand. The ability to empathise and listen to other people's arguments is advantageous. If you can persuade people to move away from their position because of the way you put your case across, you will be an asset to your organisation. Using humour appropriately is also a people skill which comes in useful from time to time.

Chapter Five:

Managing Others

'The truth of the matter is that you always know the right thing to do. The hard part is doing it.'
General Norman Schwarzkopf

Working with other people is not always easy. There is much to learn, not only about yourself but your colleagues. Should you be asked to take a position where you are responsible for others, this is an entirely different thing. Managing other people is a further development of your inter-personal skills. In this chapter there is some help and advice on how to be an effective manager.

In your current job, perhaps you were employed originally because of your core skills: scientific, financial, technical or other. Should you be technically excellent at your job and be seen to have management capabilities, you are likely to be given responsibility for others at some point. It is then that your original skills become to a large extent redundant, because what you are going to need now are management skills.

But what if you haven't got any? This could affect your career plans. Some people in this situation are lucky and get offered management training, but the vast majority are not. You have no choice but to muddle through, copy other people or emulate a role model, all of whom may have had to do precisely the same in your own past. This chapter tackles two of the foundation stones of effective management practice: delegation and appraisals – both of which are critical to developing and improving performance in others. They require advanced inter-personal skills.

Delegation

This is a word that is bandied about liberally but many do not know what it really means. People who can delegate effectively are rare. Mostly what happens is that you get *told* to do a job or take something on. Now that is not delegation. Very often it is an either/or situation. Either you get dumped with something you can't cope with, or you don't get a chance to prove your worth because delegation is not implemented effectively.

More often than not the process hasn't been thought through. This can result in things going wrong, breakdowns, upsets and so on. All very de-motivating for staff and managers alike.

If you have recently stepped up to a position of responsibility, you may be required to assign or allocate work to others in your team or department. In essence this is done by: balancing the work that has to be done:

- against the availability of the other people;
- with a view to their own abilities.

Some of the work may be routine and repetitive; other tasks may not. When you assign work to a team member, you can retain the decision-making responsibility. This is a wise move if later on it becomes necessary to decide upon an alternative course of action. Delegation could go one step further and confer the authority on the particular team member to make a decision. Learning to delegate effectively is important, because you will find your own development will suffer and you will become snowed under with work if you don't. The act of delegating work to others in your team enables you too to develop and grow.

Having said all that, there are some reasons not to delegate. Managers often feel reluctant to do it, and one of the most frequent excuses is: "It's easier to do it myself."

While that may be true to start with, it must not become the reason to avoid delegating. Soon you will find yourself in a vicious circle: the more you have to do, the easier it is to do it yourself because it is quicker than taking the time to delegate. But that road leads to overload for you and loss of morale for others. There are a number of reasons that might be preventing you from delegating. Is it that you:

- do not understand the need to delegate;
- lack the confidence with team members and, therefore, will not give them the authority for decision-making;
- do not know how to delegate effectively;
- have tried to delegate in the past, but failed and so will not try again;
- like doing a particular job which should be delegated and will not assign it to a team member even though you know he would enjoy the job;
- do not understand the management role or how to go about it;
- are frightened of making yourself dispensable, so keep hold of every job;
- have no time to delegate;
- have nobody to delegate to.

All of these barriers need to be overcome if you are to delegate effectively.

The skill of delegating

Delegation is a skill which, like any other, is one that can very quickly be learned. Most of it is common sense, but here are some tips for effective delegation:

- Plan delegation well in advance.
- Think through exactly what you want done. Define a precise aim.
- Consider the degree of guidance and support needed by delegates.
- Pitch the briefing appropriately. Check understanding.
- Establish review dates. Check understanding.
- Establish a "buffer" period at the end, in which failings can be put right.
- Delegate "whole jobs" wherever possible, rather than bits and pieces.

- Inform others involved.
- Having delegated, stand back. Do not "hover".
- Recognise work may not be done exactly as you would have done it.
- Do not 'nit-pick'.
- Delegate, not abdicate responsibility.

What should be delegated

If you are about to assign work to someone else, you must analyse the job he/she is actually doing in order to establish what can and cannot be delegated. You need to identify:

- totally unnecessary tasks which need not be done at all;
- work which should be done by another person or in another department;
- time consuming tasks not entailing much decision-making which, providing training is given, could be done as well by the team member as by the manager;
- repetitive tasks which over a period take up a considerable amount of time, but require more decision-making and would serve to help develop a team member.

A delegation plan and timetable must then be proposed to enable time to be found to delegate. Except for the simplest of jobs, you will find that something like *eight to twelve times longer* will be needed to delegate a job effectively as to actually do it. However, by taking the time to delegate properly in the first place you will save yourself far more time in the future. See it as an investment in your own future as well as in the future development of the delegate.

What should not be delegated

There are always certain tasks and authority which a manager should not delegate. This does not mean that you cannot employ staff to assist with these areas of work, but you must remain the final decision-maker. These areas of work are:

- Being forward looking and constantly seeking opportunities for the enterprise;

- Setting aims and objectives;
- Creating high achievement plans for your department or the part of it for which you are responsible, and ensuring quality standards are developed and maintained;
- Co-ordinating activity – that is knowing the task that has to be done, the abilities and needs of your own people; the resources available and then blending them to achieve optimum results;
- Communicating with your people and with senior managers and other colleagues;
- Providing leadership and positive motivation;
- The training and development of your project team;
- Monitoring and surveying everything that is going on and taking action necessary to maintain the planned level of achievement and quality performance.

From the above, it should be clear that you will not weaken your position by delegating work which does not fall into any of these areas. In fact, the contrary will be true. You will free yourself to do the jobs that you alone can do, and should do, to be effective.

How to delegate

Once a delegation plan has been prepared, each job must be taken separately. You should then prepare a specification which will state:

- the objective or intended goal of the job;
- the method you have developed to do it;
- data requirements and where the information comes from;
- any aids or equipment needed to do the work;
- the principal categories of decisions that have to be made;
- any limitations on authority given to make these decisions. Namely, when should you be consulted.

When this preliminary specification has been prepared, you must start training the delegate to do the job. Initially, close control should be maintained, but loosened as soon as possible. Some form of control must be maintained, but this should not be more than is necessary to ensure that the job continues to be done properly. Keep track of which jobs you have delegated and to whom. Monitor the process with each delegate from a tactful distance.

Delegation is often seen as being of advantage to the manager, but it is also of considerable benefit to the team member. The fact that jobs which you have developed are passed to others to do, along with the requisite authority to act, is an aid to the development of individuals, both practically and psychologically.

Delegation exercise

As you read through the list below, tick any items that you feel particularly apply to you. Then consider whether the suggested changes in what you do might be helpful.

BARRIERS TO DELEGATING	HOW YOU MIGHT TACKLE THE BARRIER
I find it difficult to ask people to do things	Try explaining to them what you will be freed to do if you take on the task
I do not have time to delegate	Decide to break out of the vicious circle and make time. By investing, say, half an hour explaining the task you save, say, the three hours it will take to do the task
It is quicker to do the job myself; explaining it to someone else takes too much time	It may be quicker to do the job yourself, but you have a responsibility to develop your staff members' skills. You will also get quicker with practice

BARRIERS TO DELEGATING	HOW YOU MIGHT TACKLE THE BARRIER
I could do the job better	Being responsible for developing the skills of your staff means investing time in development and training. In the long-run it will save time. Set up a development programme
I need to know exactly what is happening	As a manager, you must get results through other people, or you will become overloaded – so you need to trust your staff. Build in regular feedback.
I enjoy this job. I've always done it	As a manager, you have to let go of tasks that other staff can do. Do only what you can and should do
I am afraid it won't get done properly, and I will get the blame	Prepare for delegation and build in controls as the job is done. You have the right to make mistakes
I am afraid someone else will do it better than I can	Set targets for your team members to do better than you at specific tasks
You will not do it my way	Agree to goals and targets and give freedom. There are often many ways of doing a job. A good team benefits from a variety of approaches.

BARRIERS TO DELEGATING	HOW YOU MIGHT TACKLE THE BARRIER
I am not sure how to do this task so feel I had better do it myself	You need to decide how to tackle the task before deciding whether it's suitable to delegate
The job is too big/important	Break the job down. All jobs contain some routine elements which can be delegated

A good delegator or a willing martyr?

Delegation is one of the most useful things that busy people can learn.

Take the test below to see what kind of delegator you are. The answers are below.

1. What does delegation mean to you?

a) Passing the buck to juniors.
b) Dumping responsibilities.
c) Tricking others into doing work that is rightfully yours.
d) None of the above.

2. Are you nervous about delegating because:

a) You do not trust anyone else to do the work?
b) You do not want to overburden someone else?
c) You have not got time to train or prepare others?
d) Overwork is part of your job.

3. What word would you most associate with delegation?

a) Risk
b) Fear
c) Guilt
d) Trust

4. If you did delegate a task, or tasks, would they be:
a) The most boring ones?
b) The least risky ones?
c) The most risky ones?
d) The ones that a subordinate could do just as well?

5. If you had to delegate an important job to a subordinate, would you:
a) Issue it as an order?
b) Be very apologetic?
c) Leave it to someone else to convey?
d) Present it as an opportunity?

6. When delegating to someone, do you:
a) Keep worrying that the job is not being done well?
b) Ask them to report back each time a decision is made?
c) Stipulate that if anything goes wrong, it is your responsibility?
d) Tell them only to come back to you if there is a problem they cannot handle?

Effective delegation is about trusting your staff and colleagues and delegating authority – but not responsibility. (By the way, if you answered '**d**' to each question, you may need to read no further on this.)

QUESTION 1: Delegation should never be forced on others or presented in a negative way. At best it is an opportunity for career development. However much you delegate, the buck always stops with you.

QUESTION 2: If you do not trust your staff, you cannot truly delegate – you will always be involved in your judgements. It is all about learning to respect and trust your team so that tasks can be more evenly spread.

QUESTION 3: Delegation = Trust

QUESTION 4: Delegating the worst jobs is not worthy of the name.

You should delegate tasks that you would normally be able and prepared to do. It is not an excuse for offloading rotten jobs.

QUESTION 5: Good delegation needs to be presented as a positive benefit. How you "sell" delegated tasks is most important. You should delegate the interesting and challenging jobs – and negotiate with the delegate.

QUESTION 6: Learn to let go. If you trust your subordinates, let them run with a task. If you feel any doubts about your capabilities, invest in training and staff development – it's cheaper than you suffering from stress-related illness.

The second aspect of managing others covered in this chapter is performance appraisals.

Performance appraisals

A brief description follows of appraisals and their purpose. It is as useful a skill as delegating, but is often ignored or badly done. Appraisals are all too often the bane of a working life rather than something to look forward to and enjoy. Appraisals should be a win/win experience: both parties should gain by it and feel a sense of satisfaction and achievement. Here is an opportunity both for managers and staff to assess each others' performance, build a better working relationship and receive constructive feedback.

Appraisals should be conducted once a year as an absolute minimum, with less formal quarterly appraisals in the interim.

Benefits to the individual:

- Discussion of the job role in the context of job description.
- Assessing performance against agreed objectives.
- Opportunity to give and receive feedback.
- Having training needs identified.
- Opportunity to discuss career prospects and promotion.
- Future planning – understanding and agreeing objectives.
- Building relationship.

- Re-enforcing the delegation process.
- On-the-spot coaching.
- Increasing motivation and improving morale.

Benefits to the line manager:

- Evaluating performance (individual, team, organisation). Making the best use of resources.
- Giving constructive feedback .
- Setting and clarifying objectives.
- Identification of training needs.
- Audit of team's strengths and weaknesses.
- Receiving feedback on management style.
- Exploring and resolving problems.
- Reducing staff turnover.

Benefits to the organisation:

- Improved performance through commitment to their role.
- A minimum standard of good company culture.
- Sharing of skills.
- Appropriate manpower utilisation.
- Test of selection process.
- Reduce staff turnover.
- Improve morale and motivation.

Preparation for the appraisal discussion

Preparation for the interview is essential, if both parties are going to get the most out of it. You should think carefully about what you want to discuss, gather relevant information and focus on relevant issues. You will need to notify the person in writing and familiarise yourself with the individual's file and performance factors.

You will also need to think about the environment in which you conduct the appraisal. A neutral location is generally better than your office, make sure that you have what you need in the room – water, tea, coffee – ensure that you are both comfortable and that you will not be interrupted. And be sure to allow enough time.

Conducting the interview

During the Interview:

- Start on a positive note – emphasise what is working.
- Use the 10 to 1 ratio for feedback – 10 positives to 1 negative.
- Create a relaxed, positive atmosphere.
- Review the purpose of the interview.
- Use an agenda.
- Encourage the role holder to talk.
- Listen carefully.
- Use open questions.
- Keep to the agenda during the interview.
- Ensure you cover all the key aspects of the role.
- Discuss areas of improvement.
- Avoid over-criticising.
- Deal with one topic at a time.
- Summarise and maintain control throughout.
- Discuss further training and career development needs.
- Review and summarise main points, agree action plans.
- End on a positive note, thank each other for your contributions.

Here is an example of Active Listening

	ACTIVE	PASSIVE
L	Look interested	Show no encouraging responses
I	Involve yourself by questioning	Ask irrelevant questions or assume
S	Stay on target	Become distracted or daydream
T	Test your understanding	Do not clarify or summarise
E	Evaluate the message	Do not connect/relate to other information
N	Neutralise your feelings	Have prejudices and make snap judgements

After the interview, complete all documentation and confirm all agreements made during the meeting. Send these to the appraisee and copies to your HR department, as well as for your own file.

Appraisals can be opportunities for change on the one hand or they can be a damaging experience on the other. They can make the difference between high performing and motivated staff and those that do the bare minimum to get by. Which sort would you prefer?

Recruiting and selecting the right people

Something every company or organisation, whatever size, has in common – they all need staff. People are the core of any business. Some people love their jobs and others live for their work: the salesman who is driven to sell, the receptionist who enjoys meeting and greeting people. If you are aiming to be part of a happy and productive workforce, even though you may not be a recruiter of staff yourself at the moment, understanding the process puts things into context.

It is essential for any employer, when recruiting, to find and hire the best applicants. With so many people now looking for work – sometimes hundreds of candidates apply for a single vacancy – it is a big challenge for any employer to pick the best person. A word or two here on recruitment and selection might be helpful. After all, it is a vital task: get it right and everyone benefits. Get it wrong and the consequences are dire. When more hands are needed, the recruitment process should roll seamlessly forward.

Here's a brief summary of the various steps involved.

Defining the job to be done

1. Analysing the job and drafting the job description.

The creation of a clear and tangible job description is an essential first step. Investing time at this stage is a good policy. Whether the position is a new one or you are filling an existing one, before starting the recruiting process be sure you know what standards you are going to use to measure your candidates.

2. Write down the description of the job.

Is it a newly created post or an existing position? What is the job title? What are the objectives and purpose of the job? What duties, responsibilities and tasks go with it? How does it fit with existing jobs? Where will it lead and what prospects can be offered?

3. What reward package will be offered?
Make sure you are clear about the salary, benefits, holiday entitlement and all relevant information.

4. Describe the reporting lines and working relationships.
It is important that you are clear about the specific tasks, standards and responsibilities required at this stage. It is also helpful to detail the appraisal procedure.

While a clear job description is fundamental to successful recruitment, the personal profile sets out the characteristics of the kind of person who might be qualified and suited to undertake the role.

Specifying the profile of the likely candidate

1. Identifying characteristics.
This involves deciding on the qualities of the person who will be suitable for the position. Descriptions such as hard working, good attitude, experienced, stable, smart and responsible spring to mind. But finding them may take time.

2. Personal characteristics.
This covers basic personal characteristics such as age, education, experience, specialist qualifications, and other key skills such as fluency in a foreign language. The purpose here is to make the selection process manageable. Most employers wish to trawl a fairly wide area, but not hundreds of applications, most of which are unsuitable.

3. Character traits.
What sort of person would suit the vacancy? Do you want someone creative, industrious, loyal or innovative? Aspects of character, such as these, are important attributes but much more difficult to measure accurately.

Motivational factors: Will the job suit someone who wants a steady routine or someone who wants something more challenging? The manager needs to look here at what is likely to appeal to an applicant about the job. Is it suitable for someone who is ambitious, competitive, innovative and creative? These are listed as a guide only.

Responsibility: Areas of responsibility relate to the aspects of character which make a candidate suitable for the post. Does the applicant have the ability to work on his own, care for others or give presentations to large audiences? Will they need to work as part of a team? Is 100% accuracy essential in their work?

The worst-case scenario is to end up appointing someone who proves not able to do the job, but not so bad that he can be sacked. It is important to consider the kind of person you feel best suited to the position. Once you have given some time to these details, you can start the selection process.

Sources of candidates and methods of attracting the right person

From among the sources for attractive potential candidates, perhaps the most effective are:

Internal selection

Via the HR or Personnel department, internal advertisement of the position. Provided an effective training and selection programme is in place, it is possible to source and select for the new position from within the company. The advantage here is that the applicant is known to the manager, the applicant knows the company and has "bought-in" to the culture of the firm. It is good for staff morale to see that internal promotion is possible. Only after you have exhausted your internal candidates should you look outside the company.

Referrals

If you are looking to fill a vacancy, make sure you let people know. Whether it is co-workers, colleagues, friends, relative or clients – many good candidates are sourced from referrals. Someone you know might suggest an individual and give you great insights into the applicant's strengths and weaknesses and character. You will get far more information than you would from resumes alone.

Internet Advertising

If you are preparing a job advertisement, make sure the copy describes the actual job to be done, and what the organisation does in terms of its style and culture. It also needs to state clearly a specific salary range and the nature and qualifications of the candidates sought. The internet is where most people now look when searching for a job and gives you a global area from which to trawl applicants. This is advantageous but the disadvantage is that you may have to sort through literally hundreds of applications to find the good ones to shortlist.

Agencies and Recruitment Consultants

You could hire a temp. This will give you some relief if the work is piling up while the recruitment process is underway. It also provides the opportunity to try out employees before you hire them. Using an agency or recruitment consultant can save time if you cannot go through the whole process of recruitment and selection yourself. The agency carries out the advertising, recruiting and screening of applicants, providing you with a shortlist of, perhaps, five people to interview.

Executive Search/Headhunters

The higher the level of the position you are seeking to fill, then it may be appropriate to seek assistance from one of the executive search companies of headhunters. They have great experience and are able to select candidates to the highest standard.

Most applications are sent in by email, or via websites. When considering applicants' CVs bear in mind they can be quite distinctive:

- A targeted CV draws attention to the applicant's skills and focuses on the qualities that make him the right person for the particular position.

- A chronological CV is one that summarises the qualifications and career experience of the candidate. This form of CV is popular with local authorities, central government and more traditional employers.

- An experience-based CV is valid for individuals who work in specialised areas of employment. It describes their track record to date.

There is no need for large amounts of personal detail to be added to a CV. It should be a piece of personal marketing literature – focusing on the product – in other words, the skill the candidate offers. Beware ones which are gimmicky. A CV should look attractive, clean and professional. Be vigilant at checking accuracy of CVs – employment history, qualifications and skills.

Systematic approach to interview

When it comes to interviewing candidates, you do need to ask the right questions. Because hiring the right people is essential to the growth and success of your team or department, you need to get the interview techniques right. This means asking loaded questions which will reveal the information you need to make an informed decision.

At the outset, welcome the applicant, then begin by summarising the position. Ask the prepared questions and use the candidate's answers to evaluate their strengths and weaknesses. Conclude the interview after allowing the candidate the opportunity to ask any questions they wish to. Advise them that you when you will be making your selection.

Take time to prepare your questions and make notes of the applicant's answers.

"Why are you here?"

You hope the answer will reveal more than "because I want a job with your firm".

"What can you do for us?"

Some applicants approach the recruitment process on the basis of "what can your company do for me?" and this question redresses the balance.

"What kind of person are you?"

If recruited, you are likely to be spending considerable periods of time in the applicant's company. You want to employ someone who will be congenial most of the time he is at work.

"If you stayed with your current company, what would be your next move?"
This question should reveal what the applicant expects but also why the applicant wants to move on, or why he was made redundant.

"What do you consider makes you exceptional compared to others?"
A difficult question for most people. The applicant may have a good degree of self-esteem and some courage. A timid response could indicate a reticent type. Watch out for the over-active ego, this could spell disaster where teamwork is required.

"Describe your greatest achievement to date."
Any applicant who is quick enough to think on his feet and produce the answer with minimal hesitation is likely to be an asset to your company.

"Do you need many hours a week to get your work done?"
This elicits the work ethic of the potential employee. A discussion on working habits can reveal how he will fit in with the rest of the employees.

"What sort of salary are you expecting?"
There is no point in having gone through the selection process only to reach the end of the interview to discover your idea of a competitive salary and benefits package is so far removed from the candidate's vision that you are on different planets.

Keep notes as you interview each of the candidates. It will be impossible to remember who said what afterwards and your written notes will be an essential aid when evaluating the applicants.

There are one or two topics on which it is not appropriate to question applicants: these relate to the applicant's age. race, skin colour or national origin. and anything to do with marital status, religion, and criminal record. Personal details such s height, weight, financial status and disabilities are also not necessary. These questions are not relevant to how an applicant would perform their job and should be avoided.

Assessment and checks

Check, check and check again. References, skills, previous employment history. Do the dates on the CV match with other facts? It is quite surprising how many people exaggerate their education experience.

Don't be hesitant about calling previous employers for information about an applicant. You should get more detail from a supervisor or manager than from the HR or Personnel department, who is more likely simply to confirm the dates the applicant was employed.

With regard to skills, if the job requires good presentation skills, ask the applicant to give a short talk. If they need to write well, ask them to bring examples. If the requirement is for fluency in a particular language, set a test for the applicant.

Final Selection and appointment

When reviewing the information about all the candidates, how does each applicant stand up against your original criteria for the position? Is there an outright winner? How many losers? Sort them into categories: winners, possible winners and losers. Be objective. Don't be influenced by irrelevant elements such as clothes or hairstyles.

If there is more than one candidate with equally good qualifications, it may be necessary to go for a second or third round of interviews. This may seem time consuming or expensive, but it is better than making a wrong appointment and living to regret it.

If you really can't be sure – go with your gut instincts. Although they may seem equally matched in skills and experience, you will probably have a feeling that one is more suitable than the other. If so, allow your intuition free reign.

Sometimes people are hired for their personalities rather than for their skills and qualifications. Whereas it is difficult to change someone's personality, it is not impossible to teach them new skills or train them in certain techniques. Never hire someone on the basis that "They're the best of a bad bunch". This is potentially disastrous.

Once you have made your decision, telephone the successful applicant as soon as possible and offer your first choice the job and secure their acceptance. If they are no longer available, go to candidate B. Hopefully you will be able to hire someone from among your selection of "winners".

Contact the unsuccessful candidates too. A short letter to them saying you will consider them for alternatives roles (if they might suit another position in the company) or keeping their details on file is all that is required.

Remember, that new member of staff could be a manager too one day. By looking for someone who is willing to take responsibility and act on their own initiative, you could be choosing your successor.

Staff – your most valuable asset

Hold on to your assets. Most organisations know that staff hold the key to success, but not all of them capitalise on their greatest asset. Company all too often focus on making profits, increasing market share and forget that its the staff that make that happen.

Good inter-personal skills and people management keeps staff morale high. Some of the main advantages are:

- it shows an enlightened leadership culture;
- staff are actively involved at every level in the organisation;
- on-going staff development makes employees feel valued and challenged.

It costs three times as much to replace a member of staff than it does to retain one. When a company loses a key member of staff they often are the last to realise that it would have been far cheaper to tackle the issues that made that person quit, than to go through the expensive and time-consuming steps (related above) to replace them.

The greatest impact on an organisation that loses staff regularly is constantly recruiting new people. It could cost a year's salary to arrive at a "break-even" point where the new member of staff turns from being a net cost to adding value.

Consider the case of a senior manager who leaves after, say, two years' service. In replacing him the company will pay a recruitment agency, allocate HR administrators and involve directors in interviews. The two years of training investment will have disappeared. There will be loss of productivity in the run-up to his departure. His staff will be demotivated and, until his replacement is up to speed, may lose momentum and direction.

Would it not be more cost-effective to pay attention to valuable staff and retain them?

If you value your staff as tangible assets, not just overheads, you will save your organisation significant amounts of money. People make an enormous difference. What motivates and drives them to realise their potential is the way they are treated. Here are some suggestions on how to do this:

- Find some creative ways to motivate employees.
- Share knowledge with them for the benefit of the whole organisation.
- Flexible work patterns for staff who have caring responsibilities.
- Keeping work areas attractive and comfortable increases staff morale.
- Developing a praise culture shows enlightened management.

Organisations that practice good people management find it brings many benefits, including retention of key staff. Happy staff will remain with the company – surely that makes perfect sense?

Chapter Six

Surviving office politics

'Hard work spotlights the character of people: some turn up their sleeves, some turn up their noses, and some don't turn up at all.'
Sam Ewing

People mean politics. The politics-free workplace does not exist or, if it does, it 's a well-kept secret. Anyone who ignores the politics of their organisation will not hang on to their job for long, neither will they progress far. When writing about office politics, it has a predominantly negative connotation. It is easy to think of back-stabbing, plots and counter-plots, and people looking over your shoulder.

There is nothing wrong with a bit of healthy competition between colleagues, or a mix of temperaments in the workplace to stimulate creativity – but political game playing at work tends to make you think of dirty tricks. It is said that there are only three types of people in business:

- *The competent* – they rise on merit.
- *The incompetent* – they rise because of a shortage of competent people
- *The political* – they take credit from the competent while blaming the incompetent.

Although you may not be able to avoid the workplace politicians entirely, here are some suggestions on how to minimise any negative effects and advice on how to survive.

The value of gossip

If you're keen to do well in your job, you will spend time, particularly in the early days, talking to colleagues to find out how things work. When your "need to know" is all important, there's nothing like some office gossip to help fill the gaps. After all, until you've heard everything, how can you possibly decide how important the information is and whether you need to know it or not?

If you pride yourself on never wasting time at work, and certainly not being a party to chit-chat, this could be short-sighted. Conversation is the best way staff get to know each other. Relationships between people are a company's greatest asset. If colleagues don't work well together it's difficult to enjoy time spent in the workplace.

Conversation helps you connect, it is how people keep in touch with one another. If you want to be "in the know" or on the inside track, you will find out far more over a few drinks in the pub or over lunch than you will reading the staff notice board. Relaxing with your co-workers is an antidote to stress and other health problems. If you develop good social relationships at work you are far less likely to be anxious, overworked, away sick or seeking to move on. So next time you have the opportunity, join the chattering classes.

There are, on the other hand, colleagues you meet from time to time who you would like to get along with. But something tells you this is not going to happen. It causes a bit of a stumbling block – particularly if this person is in your direct reporting line. There could be a number of reasons for this – disappointment at their (perceived) lack of progress compared to yours; unhappy personal circumstances, or some other reason.

One way of tackling this issue is to pause, hold back from making any further overtures to them. Think about the way you felt about that person when you first met them.

- What initial reaction did you get?
- What sort of manner did they have?
- Did they readily make eye contact with you?

If your reaction was mostly negative, for some reason they have reservations about you and are not going to respond to you. Have a word with one or two colleagues who may know the reason why you're experiencing this problem. They may have hit this particular rock before. If not, you may have to find a way round this particular obstacle, rather than trying to move it out of the way. If they are continually ignoring or rebuffing your approaches, you have nothing to lose by letting things lapse for a while.

A piece of advice I once received was from a highly successful company director. When answering the question I had asked him, "How did you get where you are today?", he said that early on in his career he had worked hard to develop the combined skills of an acrobat, a diplomat and a doormat. The key to success, he added wryly, was knowing when, where and to what extent these skills should be used....

If you can get that right, you'll outwit the office politicians every time.

Assertiveness

Should you find yourself working with one or two colleagues who are high maintenance people or bullies, assertiveness techniques can help you out.

The key to being assertive is that in any difficult situation you leave it feeling okay about yourself and the other person involved. The aim is for a win-win outcome in terms of mutual respect and self-respect. The bonus is there's an absence of uneasiness afterwards.

The difference between being aggressive, passive and assertive is clarified this way:

- **An aggressive response** is a put down. It is a personal attack, tinged with sarcasm and arrogance.
- **A passive response** is your choice not to say or do anything confrontational. But it can leave you feeling frustrated afterwards.
- **An assertive response** is a reasonable objection which is delivered in a polite and positive manner.

If you are anxious to please, but find yourself in a tricky situation where you suspect you are being taken advantage of by a difficult colleague, you need to think on your feet. Passive behaviour in this situation gains you nothing. You can also lose a good deal from behaving aggressively.

But what happens when you behave assertively?

You feel good about yourself; you also have the satisfaction of knowing that you have handled a difficult situation correctly. There will be an absence of stress and guilt.

Here are some situations to consider – which answer would you give?

Situation 1. *Your boss asks you to work over the weekend for the second time in a month. You know the importance of the deadline and want to agree. But it's your son's fifth birthday and you've promised him you'd be home all day to help with his party.*

Solution A. You could tell your boss you've done your fair share already, having given up your previous weekend. You mention that it's not fair on your family life and can't he ask someone else.

Solution B. You could resign yourself to working and missing your son's birthday. You go home and explain, and then spend the whole of the weekend feeling resentful and guilty.

Solution C. You could say you have other commitments but offer to come in early on Monday and work late a couple of evenings that week if that would help.

Situation 2. *You've started working for a company with an established "long hours culture". This is a new experience for you and it's wearing you out. You decide, if you are going to continue with your job, that you need to cut back to a four-day week, so you prepare workable solutions to present to your directors.*

Solution A. Your suggestions are turned down so you plead with them, explaining that this is making life impossible.

Solution B. You threaten to resign if they won't compromise.

Solution C. You ask for a detailed explanation from them as to why they have rejected your proposal. Perhaps they've had a bad experience in the past with someone else who suggested a similar scenario. You rework your proposal to counter their objections and reassure them that you will not let them down.

Situation 3. *In a departmental meeting, a colleague presents one of your ideas, which you'd discussed with her a couple of days before, as her own. How do you react?*

Solution A. You say nothing because you don't want to start an argument in front of everyone. But you decide to do some straight talking to her afterwards to set the record straight.

Solution B. You express disbelief and firmly state this was your idea in the first place. You go on to say you resent being treated like this in such an underhand way.

Solution C. You diplomatically point out that it was something you and she had discussed, because you had found that this particular idea had worked well in the past. You tell the meeting how pleased you are that she's taken it on board and how much you look forward to working with her on the project.

Situation 4. *You have an urgent job to complete. You don't want to let the department down, so you ask an assistant to help you. He says he's working on an even more important assignment for someone else so he can't help.*

Solution A. You try to bribe him to fit your work in, it's something you've successfully done with others in the past.

Solution B. You try pulling rank and say there's no way this deadline can be missed. He has got to stay late and do the work.

Solution C. Explain about the urgency and tell him the reasons why the work has to be finished today. You offer to negotiate on his behalf about the other project he will have to lay aside to help you. You thank him and say you will repay the favour.

Sometimes when facing a difficult person, it's not just the person but the circumstances are also tricky. It may seem easier to postpone dealing with it, but nothing goes away if ignored. Why is it natural to put off dealing with awkward situations? There are usually three reasons

- Fear of being snubbed
- Fear of humiliation
- Fear of being rejected

But you will have to take some action. Here are the steps in order:

- *Acknowledge* that there's a problem. Don't get emotional.Take control of yourself.
- *Communicate* carefully, clearly and positively. If appropriate get support from a colleague or a superior.
- *Be flexible* in your approach and review your goals. What outcome would be best, what are you realistically likely to achieve?
- *Pay attention*, listen when engaging with the other party. Show you understand how they feel and what they are saying.
- *Analyse the problem*. It is crucial to differentiate between:
  – *the facts* (these sales figures are incorrect....)
  – *assumptions* (the calculations must have been prepared by an idiot....)
  – *generalities* (you never check your facts are right....)
  – *emotions* (how can I possibly believe you....)

- *Respond* quickly. If you can do something immediately to help, do so.
- *Focus* on this rather than the cause of past grievances.

Do not take things personally

Don't apportion blame. Don't make promises you cannot keep. If possible keep your sense of humour – laughter can lower the temperature considerably.

You are probably familiar with the expression "with friends like these, who needs enemies?". An ally in the workplace (however unlikely) is far better than a foe. When establishing working relationships, if something goes wrong in the process lose no time in getting things back on track.

A colleague could easily turn hostile if they have not been consulted about a particular change in working procedures. Perhaps they feel slighted because their views have not been sought about how things were managed in the past.

If you are the person responsible for making changes in procedures, give plenty of advance warning, Enlist team workers' help and request their views and comments. It is far easier to have a consultative phase than simply ignore people and say "we're doing it this way". Taking the temperature of the department is a good way to avoid breakdowns in communications and relationships. Staff will feel less threatened and be more likely to support you in the future.

Smoothing out problems

If you come up against some unexpected and unpleasant surprises, there are a few tips which could help. Keep calm and try the following:

Pause before you react

Don't turn a crisis into a catastrophe. Urgent problems can often be solved quite quickly. But, first of all, find out exactly what is happening. You may not have had the full story from the person who first tells you the news. Ask questions.

Use your head. (Think.)

Keep your cool. Have you ever been in a similar situation before? How did you handle it? If previous experience can aid you, a comparable solution may work this time. Otherwise you may have to get creative.

If the situation is going to need time

Create some space to deal with the problem. Cancel meetings so that you have some spare capacity. If other people are making the situation even more difficult, deal with them quickly but firmly.

Relish the unexpected

Troubleshooters are always needed. Rise to the challenge of dealing with a problematic situation. If you can sort things out, your confidence will increase and you'll be considered a great asset to your organisation.

Dealing with criticism

Some people can't resist "having a go", can they? When someone is criticising you or your performance, use your listening skills to help diffuse the situation.

- First of all, summarise the key points of their complaint.
- Outline what the other person has said to make sure you've understood correctly.
- The more specific the criticism is, the more helpful it is.
- Find out, by asking questions, exactly what action has given rise to this particular situation.
- Was it the behaviour of one person?
- What impression have they formed and why was it unfavourable?

Criticism is rarely groundless, but due to heightened emotions, can often be exaggerated. If you can swiftly extract the elements that are relevant, they can be turned to positive advantage by acting differently in future.

Always think positively and don't allow your personal hurt to cloud the issue. The people who have criticised you have alerted you to a number of things. They may not realise that not only have they given you free information but they've helped you improve your survival strategy and future planning. By implementing a solution you can take positive steps to avoid similar situations occurring and, at the same time, improve relationships with other work colleagues.

Wherever possible – give praise. Whether it is staff members who have helped you sort out the problem, or those who raised the criticism in the first place, take time to say thank you. By praising others for what they have done well or contributed, you will expertly disarm your critics. No-one ever expects to be thanked for having "dumped" on someone else. You will, at a stroke, impress people and reinforce the message that your behaviour is exemplary, even under difficult circumstances.

Checklist for coping with office politics

- ❑ Be transparent in your actions – even if other people are not.
- ❑ Communicate with all sides – and upwards as well as downwards.
- ❑ Network extensively to keep well informed – listen to gossip.
- ❑ Identify and watch the "politicians" – keep your back to the wall.
- ❑ Put yourself in other people's shoes – to see where they are coming from.
- ❑ Anticipate and manage others' reactions – be kind when others aren't.
- ❑ Be nice to people on your way up – you may need them on your way down......

Diffusing difficulties

''I don't know the key to success, but the key to failure is to try to please everybody.'
Bill Cosby

Any job is potentially stressful; if you are recently employed, or promoted, there is a lot to take on board. When your learning curve is at its steepest it pays to spot areas of potential trouble before they get serious. A glitch is easier to deal with than a problem. Never allow a situation to reach crisis point.

What may look to you like a potential problem may just be a natural part of the job. You are at times likely to have to work with unhappy or apathetic staff, angry or jealous people, those who find it difficult to tell the truth, meet obstinate cynics and cope with unreasonable bosses. This isn't bad luck; you are not being singled out. It is part of the package of life in the workplace jungle. If you can rise to these challenges and handle them calmly, you are doing well. Remember: no stress – no success. Stress is an essential ingredient when you are on the way up.

Consider these questions either for yourself or colleagues, should you be worried about stress affecting you in the workplace:

- Do you enjoy your work?
- Can you keep up with developments in your field?

- Do you get done what is expected of you on a weekly basis?
- Are you satisfied with the reward for your efforts and contribution?
- Is your relationship with your colleagues, superiors and staff reasonably good?
- Do you generally feel in control of your work?
- Can you get back on track quickly if problems or crises occur?

If the answers to these questions have mostly been "Yes", then you don't appear to be stressed. The higher the number of negatives, the more likely there is a potential problem. If you are concerned about someone, keep an eye on them for a while. See how things develop and make sure you review the situation on a regular basis.

Should their attitude or behaviour deteriorate, some action needs to be taken to bring about a solution. The better the atmosphere is among your colleagues , the less harassed you will be. People who take pride in their work have higher levels of job satisfaction and greater self-esteem. Think of it as an ever-increasing circle:

– Staff should feel the job they are doing is worthwhile.
– Management need to acknowledge that they are making a real contribution.
– This in turn helps to raise morale and job satisfaction.

Couple it with a supportive working structure and flexible work practices, and:

Teams will be productive and departments will run smoothly

If you think a member of staff is not performing well, encourage them to have an informal word with their manager. The following questions need to be asked:

- Are they feeling in control?
- Are they able to delegate?
- Are they being honest with themselves/you?
- Do they trust other peopl/ colleagues/superiors?

- Do they actually want to work with others/you/the organisation?

Depending on the answers given, the important thing to note here is how great is their negativity. The higher, the more serious the potential problem. It could be related to stress, performance or other (personal) circumstances. Whatever the reason, a remedy will be needed sooner rather than later.

Jealousy in the workplace

Should the green-eyed monster raise its ugly head in your workplace, what should you do? Job jealousy abounds and you may come up against a colleague who is desperate to cut you down as you try to make your mark.

If it's personally directed at you, rather than generally across the department, try to understand the other person's thinking. Are they resentful towards you because of your position? Maybe they had hoped to get that job themselves? Are you popular and polished while they are not? Or is there another reason? Perhaps they imagine the workplace to be fiercely competitive with only one winner. If you are perceived by them to be gaining the higher ground, their only way to cope is to push themselves forward and at the same time, try to hold you back.

If it becomes evident that where this person is concerned things like important phone messages are "forgotten", a piece of must-have information is mysteriously "mislaid", perhaps an invitation to a special event is "accidentally shredded", then be alert. Watch out too for criticisms of your work. Should any of your achievements be slighted, or there are other forms of unpleasantness occurring, it is time to take counter measures.

When dealing with envious and resentful people, do not stoop to their level or retaliate in a similar way. That only makes things worse. One way to tackle the situation is head-on. Initiate a one-to-one chat, even if you have to persist to get the person to agree. If you are refused, don't be put off, be tenacious. Open the conversation along the lines of "I feel there is some tension between us and I would like us to be able to work well together. Is everything all right?" Or, if that is too general, be more assertive and explain that when the person does X, although they may not mean to, it makes the working situation difficult and you would prefer it if they did Y. End the conversation on a positive note, such as, "Are you ok with this? Is that all right?"

If the job jealousy persists you will may have to get official and lodge a complaint. This could mean taking disciplinary action against the staff member and such processes take time. Whatever course of action you decide on, remaining professional is essential, because you will have to see the situation through.

Dealing with poor performance

This is something you may encounter from time to time. It may be useful to have a few ideas to put into practice. Here are a few options:

- Put up with it (not to be recommended).
- Re-brief or train to allow performance to improve (most favourable course of action).
- Re-assign the person to something they can do (needs their buy-in for it to work).
- Terminate employment (final solution – the necessary procedures must be followed).

These issues are linked. For example, you should only fire someone after first checking whether they are in a position to be able to do something, and providing training or whatever might help correct the situation. If no improvement then occurs, more drastic action may be necessary and justified.

Do not put off taking action because you are worrying about the reaction of others. Provided action is justified, it will almost certainly be approved. Hard-working team members hate "passengers" because usually they are the ones who have to make up the deficiencies in performance. In other words, decisive action in relation to members of the team who are letting down the rest earns you respect.

Matters of discipline

When handling staff over disciplinary issues, make sure you deal with them correctly (by that I mean procedures laid down in the Staff

Handbook). Check with superiors or the HR Department if you are in doubt. Suggested steps to take:

- Check the situation very carefully.
- If facts are not clear, check further, but do not delay long and set specific time for further action.
- Deal with the matter in hand (do not feel you have to be lenient).
- Take action and check it against policy (e.g. if a warning is necessary, should it be in writing, how should it be expressed, where should it be filed and who should be copied?).
- Remember the key task is to secure the future.
- Be fair – but do not go over the top to register your power.

Appropriate action is likely to be approved by the team. Being seen as a soft touch can create problems for the future.

Anger, frustration and other behaviour

Think, if all the people you work with worked harmoniously and efficiently all of the time, wouldn't it would be wonderful? Imagine, no complaints, no-one ever going sick or having an attitude issue. Perhaps it only occurs in films, like the *Stepford Wives*?

Reality is somewhat different. People are fallible, they behave badly some of the time and it's usually the job of the manager to sort out the problem. Staff have accountability once they accept a position of employment. They are required by their contract to maintain the standards of work and behaviour set out in their job description and company code of practice. If they trip up once or twice, perhaps a gentle reminder is all that is required. But if they fail to do what is expected of them on a regular basis, what then? In these circumstances several adverse things happen which should be addressed – effectively and fast.

First it costs the company money.
Second it upsets the balance of the workforce ("…if he gets away with it, why can't I?" sort of thing...).
Third morale plummets.
Fourth management headaches reach epic proportions.

Everyone at work is entitled to be treated with dignity and respect. Bullying, harassment and discrimination are in no-one's interests and this should not be tolerated in the workplace. If there are any signs of aggressive behaviour, someone should intervene immediately. Bullying is usually characterised as offensive, intimidating, malicious or insulting behaviour. Harassment is generally unwanted conduct affecting the dignity of men and women. Discrimination can relate to age, sex, race, disability, religion, nationality or any personal characteristic of the individual.

Should bad behaviour where you work be a potential issue, prevention is better than cure. Most companies have a definitive policy which gives staff clear examples of what is regarded as unacceptable behaviour in the organisation. You should be able to obtain from the HR Department copies of the company's policies and procedures for dealing with grievance and disciplinary matters. Make yourself familiar with them and, if necessary, consult with others in your peer group as to whether there have been past cases and what the outcomes were.

Any employee should know who they can refer to if they have a work-related behavioural problem. This is a sensitive area and should you be encountering it for the first time check whether the member of staff who is being bullied or harassed is overreacting to something fairly trivial. Don't judge the situation from your own viewpoint. It could be that this is the "last straw" for a member of staff following a long series of unreported incidents.

The danger, where such behaviour goes unchecked, is that it creates serious problems for the organisation as a whole, such as:

- poor morale
- unharmonious staff relations
- loss of respect for management
- bad performance
- low productivity
- absences
- resignations

All of these seriously damage the company's reputation and results. Should you discover that a colleague makes frequent mistakes, exhibits inappropriate behaviour or their performance standards fall way short of the company policy, this is not acceptable. They are showing contempt for the company by not caring about their work, or behaviour. The effect this has on the organisation and how their behaviour impacts on their colleagues is detrimental.

Hopefully, the person you report to does not take the ostrich approach (…..head up backside…) and hopes matters improve. A problem rarely gets smaller by being disregarded. What starts as a minor dispute can develop into a full-blown crisis if ignored. Confront the issue, or the situation will only get worse.

It is worth noting that discipline should not to be confused with punishment. Discipline is positive; punishing someone is to do with exacting a penalty.

Effective discipline involves dealing with the shortcomings or misconduct before the problem escalates. Depending on the severity of the problem, disciplining an employee can be an informal or formal procedure. If an informal approach is appropriate, counselling or training can provide a vital role in resolving complaints.

Whichever the case, it is important that a fair procedure is followed. When the issue involves a complaint about bullying, harassment or discrimination, there must be fairness to both the complainant and the person accused.

Whether you are the "whistle-blower", the recipient of the behaviour or the manager who is dealing with the complaint, time should not be allowed to elapse between the incident taking place and disciplining the staff member as appropriate. If this happens the message being sent is weak – no-one could be bothered to do much about it.

Standards of behaviour in most organisations are set by means of a statement which is given to all staff when they join or through the company handbook. Any complaints of bullying, harassment or discrimination must be dealt with fairly, confidentially and sensitively, as laid down in the company manual. Because of recent changes in the law, it is essential to seek professional advice on good practice in disciplinary matters. This should avoid cases escalating and ending up before employment tribunals. You have been warned...

Chapter Seven

Focusing on key issues

'Even if you're on the right track – you'll get run over
if you just sit there.'
Arthur Godfrey

A person who successfully relates to others, and can deal sympathetically with all of their colleagues, is a valuable asset to any organisation. This type of person doesn't spend time learning how to *talk* but learning how to *listen*. People who are aware of others are likely to live and work in harmony; so take time to understand those with whom you work.

If you don't, colleagues can become increasingly demanding or disgruntled. It works both ways: if your co-workers don't have a clue, or care, about where you stand, it will make you feel worthless and unimportant. Everyone needs to be valued and appreciated – this is the professional approach to working successfully with others.

If you can position yourself within your organisation as someone with the right attitude, able to embrace change, who wants to help and get along well with others, you will be seen to be outward looking. Develop strengths such as:

- reliability
- honesty
- integrity
- patience

Research has proved that people with successful personal relationships are happier, healthier and live longer. Those who can coexist peaceably at work suffer less stress, are more effective and productive, as well as gaining more workplace satisfaction. To be able to get along with colleagues and be successful in dealing with people you should show interest and respect for others. Then allow them time to do the same for you.

What has been covered in this book explains that when working with other people, respect their differences and be courteous and polite where possible. Bad manners does not help keep a diverse group of individuals united, whatever the work is.

Skills such as problem-solving, negotiation and persuasion will help you in your work. Should you have to manage others, remember that motivated individuals are more positive and will work better and be more productive.

There is no doubt that the importance of clear communication is paramount. Where there is ambiguity or doubt progress cannot be made. Much has been written about communication styles and methods and it is worth paying attention to this should you feel your skills are weak in this area. It is only by persuasiveness that you can maintain problem-free working relationships when changes need to be made. Smooth operators go far and will take others forward with them. Look out for any you meet and emulate them when opportunities occur.

People matter – there's no doubt about it. People – unlike tasks – cannot be hurried. Short cuts are sometimes fine but when working well with others matters make sure there is enough time. If you are occasionally in doubt about how to deal with someone, just think how you would wish to be treated should the roles be reversed. Whether it is recruiting, selecting, mentoring, motivating, appraising, promoting – getting it right is essential. Get it wrong and it can take ages to recover from very costly mistakes. Team building is a science in itself and good team leaders know this only too well.

Behaviour and performance are important whatever industry you work in. Take care of yourself, and keep an eye on those with whom you work. Stress up to a point is positive, but over a certain level it becomes dangerous. Time management skills and personal effectiveness among individuals are highly desirable qualities so keep yours in good repair.

Take advantage of any training courses that are offered along the way – there is always something that can be learned or reviewed.

Methods to take you onwards and upwards

Maintaining credibility

If you act like you mean to go on, people will believe in you and respect what you do. Remember:

- You are not judged by the number of times you fail, but by the number of your successes. Keep an eye on the ratio.
- You are more likely to succeed by sticking your neck out than always playing it safe. Show consideration and take care.
- If you admit your mistakes, people will see you are human. They may even be prepared to help you not to repeat them (and avoid making similar ones themselves).
- You should never cut other people out until it is unavoidable. You never know what changes may occur.

Accepting change

Embrace change. Change happens (this could be related to new technology, work processes and practices, and personnel) and there's not much you can do about it. Some people ignore it, others try to stop it. If you want to work successfully with others, there may be some who are fighting the inevitable and resisting change. There are four phases through which people pass before they embrace change. These are:

Denial: "That's never going to work", "We don't need them". Are there any ostriches in your organisation? They may have their heads in the sand, but change is not going to go away as a result of their not seeing it.

Resistance: Some people try to stick with the old ways of doing things. "But it's always worked ok in the past when X did it." The reality is, the sooner you get to grips with new methods, the better it is for your career (and your blood pressure).

Exploration: Maybe the change doesn't have to be all bad. Is it possible that there are some advantages to the new way of working/new people on the team? If you look at the change with a more open mind, you may begin to find some good things that come from it.

Acceptance: Once you reach this stage, you may even find that the new systems/staff work better than you'd believed possible. You have by this time fully integrated the change into your own routine.

There are a number of things people do to cause difficulty at work.

- Use old methods of working when they should be playing by the new rules.
- Avoid taking on new assignments for fear that they might have to work in a different way.
- Try to slow things down to their own pace. Unfortunately change usually requires people to speed up, so they risk getting left further and further behind.
- They play the victim/martyr role. Unfortunately more flexible colleagues won't show them any sympathy.
- Trying to control the uncontrollable. This is a bit like attempting to stop the tide from coming on to the beach. Change is inevitable – they'll have to accept it. Instead of wasting energy resisting, they should go with the flow.

You may be working with colleagues whose behaviour is similar to that described above. Their difficulty lies in their entrenched attitude. Don't resist change yourself. If you can show a willingness to embrace it, you will be noticed as an asset to your organisation. You're a smooth operator and your receptiveness is your passport to future success.

And finally.........

Anyone is capable of getting on well with others if that is what they *want* to do, provided they know the way to do it. Motivation and energy is the currency needed to harness people-power. In terms of career management and self-development, workplace relationships are an inevitable and constantly changing part of life.

With all that has been covered in this book, how can you ensure that your people skills will continue to develop? How will you make the right choices and get satisfaction from working with others? If you take responsibility for your actions from the outset, you must recognise your strengths and weaknesses. You will need to monitor your progress and find yourself a mentor if necessary to help you along.

You have probably discovered by now that successfully working with other people does not just happen. Success is not a given – you have to invest in it. Those who succeed in developing strong inter-personal skills often say that what they achieve is directly related to the amount of effort they put in (in themselves, in others). Among the things that will help you are:

- Keeping a positive attitude;
- Seeing where your skills need to be extended or upgraded;
- Being genuinely interested in others;
- Making good contacts everywhere you go;
- Analysing what your strengths are and how you are doing.

If you think that the effort you have to put in to become a smooth operator with colleagues is far greater than you imagined, don't forget that it gets easier the more practice you have. What is needed is an attitude of optimism: one that assumes you will make progress (even if the obstacle seems insurmountable). Have courage, take action and see what you can achieve. You may be pleasantly surprised.

Frances Kay

With many years work experience, covering politics, diplomatic service and law, Frances has helped professional individuals and organisations on all aspects of career and personal development, and relationship building. The majority of her time is now spent writing business books and articles, researching, editing and giving interviews, talks and workshops on her book topics.

Four years ago Kogan Page Publishers appointed Frances Kay Editor of their bestselling title *The Good Non Retirement Guide*, an annual publication. The 26th edition appears in January 2012. The book covers every aspect of retirement, from managing money, health, property, making the most of your leisure to starting and running your own business.

Since turning 60 herself, Frances has relished the challenges and opportunities that this project has involved. Frances also spends time helping entrepreneurs and small businesses on a pro-bono basis – particularly those located in Gloucestershire.

Other Books in Smart Skills Series

Mastering the Numbers

Meetings

Negotiation

Persuasion

Presentations

www.smartskillsbooks.com

www.legendpress.co.uk

www.twitter.com/legend_press